M000306796

A DOSE OF HOPE

A Dose of Hope

A STORY *of* MDMA-ASSISTED PSYCHOTHERAPY

Dr. Dan Engle & Alex Young

Cautions and conditions on reading *A Dose of Hope*:

The authors would like to alert the readers that *A Dose of Hope* is for informational purposes only and simply intended to convey an understanding of the background, current state of research, and potential benefits of MDMA as a therapeutic agent. This is not an endorsement of independent personal use of MDMA, recreationally or therapeutically, outside of government-sanctioned research. Currently, it is a criminal offense in the United States and in many other countries, punishable by imprisonment and/or fines, to manufacture, possess, supply, or utilize MDMA for any reason outside of a legally sanctioned clinical trial.

Furthermore, the information provided here does not constitute the practice of medicine, psychotherapy, or any other professional healthcare service, including the giving of medical advice. The use of information in this book is at one's own discretion. The contents of this book are not intended to be a substitute for professional medical advice, diagnosis, or treatment. Readers should not disregard or delay in obtaining medical or therapeutic advice for any personal health condition they may have and should seek the assistance of their healthcare professionals for any such conditions.

The authors and the publisher expressly disclaim any liability, loss, or risk, personal or otherwise, that is incurred as a consequence, directly or indirectly, of the contents of this book.

COPYRIGHT © 2021 DR. DAN ENGLE & ALEX YOUNG
All rights reserved.

A DOSE OF HOPE
A Story of MDMA-Assisted Psychotherapy

ISBN   978-1-5445-2103-9 *Hardcover*
       978-1-5445-2102-2 *Paperback*
       978-1-5445-2101-5 *Ebook*

LIONCREST
PUBLISHING

To my sister Trudy, whose passing became my call to action.

Thank you for your fierce love in the midst of unspeakable odds.

May each of us suffering in silence

remember that the caterpillar has yet to fathom

what it's like to be a butterfly.

Contents

Introduction

In the United States, during the time it takes you to finish this book, approximately 125 people will take their own lives.

The mental health crisis plaguing our culture today does not stop with suicide. The epidemics of depression, anxiety, PTSD, addiction, and chronic pain are simply expressions of a psychiatric system that is largely devoid of effective methods to deal with the deeper issues underlying the symptoms.

Namely, these underlying issues are core emotional wounds, unmet needs of the psyche, isolation or disconnection from one another, a lack of faith in something greater than one's own self, nervous systems stuck in fight or flight, and the empty promises of material success, to just name a few.

This is not to imply the current psychiatric field is wrong—it's just incomplete. Current pharmaceuticals have their place when symptoms are severe and need to be relieved. However, they should only be instituted while still looking at the deeper causative factors and working to resolve them.

We have another tool that can greatly help alleviate so much suffering that our current system does not address. And in the specific case of chronic, severe PTSD, the data is incontrovertible—this tool works.

That tool, broadly speaking, is **MDMA-assisted psychotherapy.**

PTSD stands for Post-Traumatic Stress Disorder. In its classic and severe form, it has been known in the field of combat experience as "shell shock" and "concentration camp syndrome," and this stems from catastrophic exposure to life-threatening events. Today, that relatively limited definition has been expanded to include a wider demographic of people who have experienced a more varied trauma history, where their significant symptoms have still left them severely compromised.

When it comes to treating chronic, severe PTSD, the current standard of care model (psychotherapy and medication management) has a roughly 35 percent improvement rate.[1]

Compare this to chronic, severe PTSD treated with MDMA-assisted psychotherapy. It has roughly a 70 percent cure rate ("cure" here is defined as the patient no longer meeting the criteria for PTSD).[2]

At face value, that sounds pretty good as it appears to double

---

1   Bradley D. Grinage, "Diagnosis and Management of Post-Traumatic Stress Disorder," *American Family Physician* 68, no. 12 (December 15, 2003), https://www.aafp.org/afp/2003/1215/p2401.html. Laura E. Watkins, Kelsey R. Sprang, and Barbara O. Rothbaum, "Treating PTSD: A Review of Evidence-Based Psychotherapy Interventions," *Frontiers in Behavioral Neuroscience* (November 2, 2018), https://doi.org/10.3389/fnbeh.2018.00258. Olivia Metcalf, et al., "Treatment augmentation for posttraumatic stress disorder: A systematic review," *Clinical Psychology: Science and Practice* 27, no. 1 (December 22, 2019), https://doi.org/10.1111/cpsp.12310.

the benefit rate. Except it's better than that. MDMA-assisted psychotherapy is orders of magnitude better.

A mild to moderate improvement is better than nothing to be sure, but it still means the symptoms are present, and they are negatively impacting the person's life in a significant way. The key is the difference between "improvement" and "cure."

A cure in this context means a person no longer has symptoms meeting the criteria for even having PTSD at all. So we are roughly going from a 35% "improvement" rate to a 70% "cure" rate.

This is not a small change. This is as big as it gets in the field of mental health.

No other tool known to the world today has as much potency and potential to help people heal trauma—and instigate change in their lives—than MDMA-assisted psychotherapy.

Sound promising? It is. Hugely.

That is what this book is about.

It is intended to offer you information on one of the most powerful mind-healing agents on the planet right now.

---

2 Allison A. Feduccia, et al., "Breakthrough for Trauma Treatment: Safety and Efficacy of MDMA-Assisted Psychotherapy Compared to Paroxetine and Sertraline," *Frontiers in Psychiatry* (September 12, 2019), https://doi.org/10.3389/fpsyt.2019.00650. Marcela Ot'alora G., et al., "3,4-Methylenedioxymethamphetamine-assisted psychotherapy for treatment of chronic posttraumatic stress disorder: A randomized phase 2 controlled trial," *Journal of Psychopharmacology* 32, no. 12 (October 29, 2018), https://doi.org/10.1177/0269881118806297. Lisa Jerome, et al., "Long-term follow-up outcomes of MDMA-assisted psychotherapy for treatment of PTSD: A longitudinal pooled analysis of six phase 2 trials," *Psychopharmacology* 237 (August 2020), https://doi.org/10.1007/s00213-020-05548-2

As of the writing of this intro, MDMA is not legal to use in therapy outside of carefully run, very small clinical trials. Thankfully though, MDMA therapy is steadily working its way through the very last stage of the DEA's federal requirement process to become a legally available treatment for people throughout the nation. As it looks now, we are on track for a greater expansion roll out increase by the end of 2021 and through 2022 to meet the demand of the people.

It's an incredible time for the field of mental health and wellness. We've never been this close to delivering such powerful healing agents to the masses, and I couldn't be more excited.

I'm so inspired, in fact, that I have dedicated my life to being part of the process that helps medicines like MDMA become widely available and better understood.

Yes, I want to do this for the obvious reason: it will help a lot of people.

But there's more to it for me—a set of more personal reasons.

I struggled with severe depression and, at one time, contemplated taking my own life. It was a medicine similar to MDMA that helped me get unstuck and pulled me out of that state.

My sister Trudy was not so lucky. In 2013, she committed suicide.

This is the major impetus for me to co-write this book.

Like many family members of suicide, I'm not even sure how to write about it. To do it full justice and tell the whole story would require volumes. Here are the "highlights" of it:

She's eight years older than me (it still feels demeaning and strange to write about her in the past tense) and my half-sister. We share the same father and were raised in separate households. Even though we saw each other less than if we had grown up down the hallway, we still felt the deep, soul-level connection of siblings that exists across space and time.

As a child, she was witty, feisty, rebellious, and sincere. As an adult, she was deep, powerful, passionate, and brooding. She was first and foremost a poet and poured her heart out through her writing. This is one of my favorite poems of hers:

Masks
the wind silently
calls for me
urging me
to go on,
it picks me up
and carries me
to the place
where I belong.
and when I remove
this false disguise
only you my friend
will see,
the person you have
known so long
is in fact—
not even me...

Years later, during my studies in psychiatric medicine, she revealed to me the source of her poetry and her pain: repeated sexual abuse as a child.

While being raised in her mother's household, she was serially molested by an uncle. This occurred frequently and regularly from her elementary school years into middle school.

Like so many victims of child abuse, she was consumed by shame and guilt and, thus, hid this truth. Nobody on our father's side knew back then. We're not sure if anyone knew what was going on outside of Trudy and her abuser.

She used alcohol to help numb the pain. And poetry. Poetry helped give it a voice. And to relieve it.

She did all the "right things" in the standard medical treatment: mountains of psychotherapy, a litany of antidepressants, and biweekly AA meetings. She was committed to living fully, went to church faithfully, and helped others whole-heartedly.

Then, one night, after fourteen months of sobriety, with a bottle of wine and a gun—and no warning signs—she ended her life.

We still don't know why and may never uncover the reason. She must have been suffering heroically for a long time and the inescapable pain finally overtook her.

Addiction was not the problem. Addiction was her strategy to cope with her trauma.

Most people can't comprehend the magnitude of suffering required to actually take one's own life. You have to live it to know it. It's an abyss that can feel impossible to get out of.

This was a lightning strike for me. It was my call to action.

This is why it's my mission to educate, advocate, and facilitate the implementation of psychedelic therapies, beginning with MDMA-assisted psychotherapy, into the medical mainstream.

This book is the latest installment in service to this mission, and it was written to help you, the layperson, become educated on this therapy.

This book also exists because of how well MDMA therapy helped a friend of mine. Over many years, I've supported and facilitated a number of people in their journey to become educated and experienced in MDMA-assisted psychotherapy. One of those people is a famous novelist. She had a series of sessions that helped her systematically reconcile her underlying trauma, and through this profoundly positive change, she felt deeply called to give back and help others find their healing.

She came to me with an idea for a book. She envisioned a story about a regular guy who gets called to MDMA-assisted psychotherapy. She saw the lead character not as a war veteran or a rape victim or someone who'd suffered severe and acute trauma. Although the primary research is being done on severe PTSD victims—and those people should be the first recipients of therapy—they would already be primed to receive its benefits. As she saw it, the big-picture vision was making the storyline relevant to the masses. This was especially important to her, considering that when she found this work, she didn't think she had much trauma, if any at all. (It turns out she was quite wrong.)

Initially, I was uncertain of this approach. I'd been so focused on helping acute trauma survivors and telling Trudy's story that I hadn't given much consideration to telling the larger story—that trauma is not just an individual issue affecting a few unlucky people: *it's a collective one that applies to all of us.*

Most everyone in our culture is living through some sort of trauma, directly or indirectly. Whether it's through first-hand experience of it themselves, witnessing it in a loved one, receiving the transgenerational expression of trauma from their families, or via other means, trauma is all around us, and we're all affected.

Data move science, politics move law, but it is a story that moves culture. So, I decided to work with her to help tell a story that can explain this work and move our culture further towards it, and this book is the result.

A Dose of Hope is a parable of healing that shares both the science and the personal experience of MDMA-assisted psychotherapy through the character of Alex Young.

Though this therapy is not yet broadly legal, the book takes place when it is so (likely eighteen to twenty-four months from this writing).

The character of Alex is, of course, not a real person. He's based on both the experience of the author and interviews done with many other people who've gone through MDMA-assisted psychotherapy.

You meet Alex as he comes to his first appointment with me to discuss the therapy. You will learn everything he learns, as he learns it, and follow his experiences as he goes through the MDMA-assisted psychotherapy process.

Though you'll get access to Alex's experiences, we decided not to spend much time exploring Alex's internal monologue, nor did we fully develop Alex's character, as would happen in a regular novel. We'd rather you, the reader, see Alex as a stand-in for yourself (or someone you know) and we felt the best way to do that was allow space in Alex for you to project yourself into him.

The novel was written in a dialogue format for that same reason—to enable you, the reader, to put yourself into Alex's shoes and experience as much as possible and not overburden you with too much information about him, so that you can ask yourself what the experience would be like for you.

We also decided to write this parable style, with a simple, straight-forward plot and an informational story—again, to allow you, the reader, to focus on learning about the therapy.

In short, don't expect literary fiction. Expect to learn and feel and explore yourself.

We also took pains to ensure people would understand the intensity of the experience and how serious this is. This medicine is not a panacea or a silver bullet. It does not magically make everything go away. Rescuing someone from their own healing work is similar to robbing someone of their greatest teacher. Preparation and integration are as critical to the success of the treatment as the experience itself.

The most important goal of the book is to teach information, reveal insights, and answer key questions that a reader interested in MDMA-assisted psychotherapy might have. For example:

Why does someone decide to do MDMA-assisted psychotherapy?

What's it actually like?

What's integration work, and why is that important?

How does it work in practice?

What's trauma?

Why does anyone need to care?

How do you heal from it?

The book shows how an average person would come to answer these very difficult and complicated questions.

My hope is that this book can reach those who are suffering and show them a way out.

There is always hope, and this is a story of how hope can turn into action and maybe save a life.

CHAPTER 1

Alex Questions Dr. Dan

The clinic was located in a gray two-story townhouse at the edge of a forest and looked like any other medical office. Flute music played in the background as I walked into the candlelit lobby, which smelled sweet and woody, like a spa, but without the humidity.

I told the receptionist my name; she said they were expecting me. I'd already filled out the primary questionnaire online, so she gave me a bottle of water and told me Dr. Dan would be ready for me soon.

I sat in the waiting room, flipped through a magazine, not really reading it, and realized something: *I was nervous.*

I kinda laughed because—*what am I nervous about? This is just a consultation. I'm not committed to anything.*

Besides, why would I be nervous about taking MDMA? I took it in college once. I know what it's like. What's the worst that could happen?

The receptionist told me Dr. Dan was ready and walked me back to a small office. Dr. Dan stood to greet me as I walked in. He was about 5' 9" and slim but in a healthy, active way. He was dressed in comfortable but stylish workout clothes, had a freshly shaved bald head, and seemed to radiate warmth and kindness. He was not dressed like any doctor I'd ever met, almost like he'd just come back from a hike.

He gave me a warm handshake, and I sat down in the chair across from him and rubbed my hands on my pants. I was even more nervous that I'd been in the waiting room, and I still didn't understand why.

Dr. Dan: "Alex, nice to meet you. I understand you're possibly interested in MDMA-assisted psychotherapy?"

Alex: "Yeah, maybe."

Dr. Dan: "I find that, for most people, it's best to begin with your questions. It helps me get a clear understanding of where you are and what you expect. Does that work?"

Alex: "Yeah, sure."

Dr. Dan: "Good. Please feel free to ask me anything. We'll take as long as you need to get all your questions answered."

I've never had a doctor say we have as much time as we need for questions.

Alex: "Maybe this isn't relevant—"

Dr. Dan: "Any question you have is relevant. An important part of therapy is feeling safe, and safety for many people is rooted in understanding. So, please, ask away."

Alex: "How did MDMA even become used for this kind of therapy? I mean, it was an illegal drug when I took it in college, right?"

Dr. Dan: "The history of MDMA is really interesting. It was discovered in 1912 by a chemist working for Merck, but no one really understood how it worked until a man named Alexander Shulgin, a chemist working for Dow at the time, independently synthesized it in 1965.

"Shulgin tested it on himself, thought it had promise, and gave it to a psychotherapist friend of his named Leo Zeff. Zeff realized it had great potential as an aide for psychotherapy, because it lowered people's inhibitions and gave them a deeper access to themselves.

"In the '70s and '80s, Zeff went on to travel the world and trained thousands of therapists on how to use this compound in their therapy, to great effect."

Alex: "Oh wow. If it started out being used in therapy, how did it become illegal?"

Dr. Dan "Well, as this was going on, some other people started using MDMA as a party drug, and it came to be known as Ecstasy. It was caught up in the massive anti-drug campaigns of the '80s and made a Schedule 1 drug, which means the federal government declared it had no medicinal purpose.

"That was very unfortunate because it clearly had medicinal

use and was being used by thousands of psychotherapists, and many of the early studies were quite promising.

"After being put into Schedule 1, its use was super restricted, and essentially, it went underground.

"From there, an organization called MAPS spearheaded the effort to do double-blind, placebo-controlled trials to make MDMA legal again.

"The studies showed incredible promise, and after many years of effort, in 2017, MDMA was granted 'breakthrough therapy' designation for PTSD by the DEA.

"After the astonishing results of the Phase 3 trials, it's now legal to use with a prescription and in controlled settings like this one, of course."

Alex: "I had no idea it's been in use that long."

Dr. Dan: "Most people don't."

Alex: "How does MDMA work, as a medicine?"

Dr. Dan: "It's the best compound we know for dealing with trauma because it does three primary things in the brain: First, it relaxes the fear center. Second, it helps you achieve heightened self-awareness in the observation part of the brain. Third, it improves your level of connection between the memory center in the hippocampus and the observation part of the brain.

"What all this means is that we're able to be less guarded and more available to see the truth, and we have a better memory of when the truth got shut down. Once your brain gets into this state, then it's able to bring up and feel deeply repressed and difficult emotions.

"You create the space for the emotions; you allow them to come up; you process what you need to feel about them, learn from them, and then you're able to let them go. Does that make sense?"

Alex: "Yeah, I think so. What will it feel like when I take it as part of therapy?"

Dr. Dan: "When you took Ecstasy in college, what did it feel like?"

Alex: "Pretty amazing. I felt good, I danced a lot, and I had this really blissful experience. I felt really terrible the next day though, so I never took it again."

Dr. Dan: "How do you respond to caffeine and other stimulants?"

Alex: "Normally. Some more energy—that's about it."

Dr. Dan: "Okay, good. MDMA usually feels like you drank a double espresso. Your heart rate and blood pressure will go up some. You'll probably feel the sensation of warmth as it starts to come on. From there, it generally creates a feeling of love, wellbeing, and safety."

Alex: "Yeah, I remember that love feeling. I kept wanting to hug people."

Dr. Dan: "Therapeutically is very different than recreationally, mainly because of the set and setting.

"MDMA is an empathogen, which means it helps us get in touch with our experience of love and interpersonal connection. Most people feel more love than they've ever felt before.

"Some people will feel it and be unsure, like they're not sure they can trust that love, because they are not used to it. Or the flip side of that might be like, 'Holy shit, this feels so right.'

"Occasionally you can have visual experiences, though that's not typical. MDMA is not technically a psychedelic in a chemical sense, so it usually doesn't have that visionary landscape.

"Most commonly, it leads you into a deep experience in your body. You get in touch with yourself, with old traumas or injuries or areas in your body that you've been cut off from—things like that. You become more aware of and connected to your emotions and feelings."

Alex: "How safe is it?"

Dr. Dan: "When used properly, it's one of the safest known pharmaceuticals.

"The LD-50, which is the dose at which half the people taking it would die and a common measure of toxicity, is orders of magnitude higher than the therapeutic dose. You'd have to take hundreds of times more than what we administer to be at risk. So, there's essentially no risk there.

"One potential danger is if someone has severe heart issues, like very high uncontrolled blood pressure or advanced heart disease that has caused heart attacks in the past or required surgery. This risk is related to MDMA increasing blood pressure and heart rate. People with the issues that arise from an elevated heart rate should avoid it, but you said on your intake form you've never had any heart issues like a heart attack or irregular heartbeat, so you should be fine.

"There are rare issues with liver disease making it challenging to metabolize the medicine. Also, if you're prone to chronic, severe, and poorly controlled seizures, taking MDMA could make it more likely to have another episode, but your screening indicates that you don't have those issues.

"One big potential danger comes if you take MDMA when you are on antidepressants or MAOIs. MDMA essentially acts in the opposite way that antidepressants do. If you take MDMA while on those compounds, it can cause some serious problems, including what is called serotonin syndrome, and even in very rare cases, death. But you said you aren't taking any antidepressants or MAOIs, correct?"

Alex: "Right. I was on Paxil after college for a few months, but I didn't like it, so I stopped. That's not a problem, is it?"

Dr. Dan: "Not at all. For most of those medicines, it usually only takes about six weeks to get them out of your system and back to normal. You're many years away from that, so you're fine."

Alex: "Could I have a bad trip on MDMA?"

Dr. Dan: "When you say 'bad trip,' what exactly do you mean?"

Alex: "You know, like, when people freak out on drugs. I've seen people having bad trips at concerts and places like that. It's scary to watch."

Dr. Dan: "I have as well, and you're right: it can be frightening. But the likelihood of that type of experience happening is very slim.

"Most of those sorts of 'bad trip' experiences happen because the person was taking a medicine that they didn't understand, or they took too high of a dose, or were in a really uncontrolled environment.

"This is different. This is a therapeutic process. We're working with really clear, clean medicine, in a specific dose range and in a highly controlled environment, with trusted specialists and an educated patient consciously choosing to do this work.

"If all of those things are taken care of—if you can trust the facilitation—if you can trust the medicine, then you can trust the process."

Alex: "So, you're saying I should be fine?"

Dr. Dan: "Physically, yes, absolutely.

"But let me be clear: even with complete physical safety, the process can still be very intense and uncomfortable for some people. And many people consider that intensity and discomfort to be a 'bad trip.'

"So, in a sense, a 'bad trip' is only bad because you weren't ready for the intense emotions and experiences that come up. If you're ready, or if you're willing to surrender to them, it's good. It's what you came for. Does that make sense?"

Alex: "I think so, yeah."

Dr. Dan: "I'd even say, in a trusted, safe space, a 'bad trip' is usually the best trip. Because it brings up the stuff that we've been avoiding for a long time."

Alex: "I don't understand that. A 'bad trip' is good?"

Dr. Dan: "Yes, in a sense. Do you lift weights?"

Alex: "Yeah."

Dr. Dan: "What are the best workouts? The ones that produce the best results for you?"

Alex: "The hardest ones."

Dr. Dan: "Exactly right. But why do they produce the best results?"

Alex: "Because that's how you get in shape. You have to stress your muscles and tear them down, so they can grow back stronger."

Dr. Dan: "Exactly. And in a metaphorical sense, that's how 'bad trips' work. When deep and intense emotions come up, that's actually the point of MDMA therapy.

"It could be trauma that comes up. It could be the recognition of the most shameful thing you've ever done, that you didn't want anybody else to know, and you didn't even want to fully acknowledge or remember that you did.

"It could be the way that your heart was broken, and the most uncomfortable way that then shaped how you started to guard.

"The least desirable emotions to feel and face can be our best teachers, if we're willing to listen to them. Many people would call those 'bad trips,' but in my experience, they are how we do the best work."

Alex: "This happened to you? You've had 'bad trips'?"

Dr. Dan: "Oh yes. Many. I've had some really uncomfortable experiences, stuff that spun me out or led me to question everything in my life, including myself. It wasn't easy, and it wasn't pretty."

Alex: "Does this happen to people on MDMA?"

Dr. Dan: "Sometimes, yes.

"But let me clear: if you're in the experience, and you're having a freak-out, I want you to know I'm going to be right there. I've worked with a lot of people going through really heavy shit. I've gone through really heavy shit myself, so I understand how to do it and how to guide you through it.

"We'll work through it together, and you'll get to a better place eventually."

I'd never really had anyone talk to me like that in my life: bluntly honest but so gentle and kind and understanding.

And for real—what doctor admits to having 'bad trips'! That's kind of crazy but also weirdly awesome.

I decided to see how open Dr. Dan would be with me.

Alex: "I'm not sure if I'm allowed to ask this, but have you done MDMA therapy?"

Dr. Dan: "That's a totally fair question, and one I would ask in your position. Yes, I have. Several times. You kind of have to in order to do this work."

Alex: "What was it like? What happened?"

Dr. Dan: "I found myself very open and free, able to just sit back and relax my mind and get more curious about myself.

"I looked at the ways in my life that I play it safe or that I am rude to people. I really looked at how I've been a jerk to some people I cared about. I saw the ways that I wasn't fully in love in my past relationships.

"This stuff just started coming out in a rush. I just started voice recording it, and then I had, like, fifty things to reflect on afterwards.

"For example, I was married once, and I was a real asshole to my wife. I saw that and felt it, and it was painful to face.

"I thought about how I'd had sex when I was way too young, and that was super confusing. I was just trying to find a real connection, and I had to ponder what the hell else was going on in my life that I'd do that.

"It was an intense process for me. It taught me more than most of the previous work talk therapy alone had done.

"What's wrong? You look a bit perplexed."

Alex: "I've never heard a doctor talk like this. You're just…so… honest."

Dr. Dan: "Part of doing the work is having to be honest with yourself, and once you do that, you find it easier to be honest and authentic with others. I don't have to share this if it's not interesting to you."

Alex: "Oh no, it is…I just wasn't expecting this. You're the first doctor I've ever heard call himself an 'asshole.'"

Dr. Dan: "Well, I really *was* an asshole to her.

"Alex, I feel it's important for me to be honest with my patients. After all, if you do this therapy, it will require you to be honest with yourself and with me, and that requires trust. I'm willing to share parts of me if it helps you trust me and, thus, go deeper in your therapy. What other questions do you have?"

Alex: "How much experience do you have sitting for people on MDMA?"

Dr. Dan: "I'm honestly not sure on the precise number; I'd have to look it up, but I know I've sat for at least five hundred people."

Alex: "Wow. That's a lot."

Dr. Dan: "This is my life's work."

Alex: "Is this addictive?"

Dr. Dan: "If we're talking about MDMA, then yes, people have gotten addicted to it, for sure. But really only in a recreational setting.

"You'll be doing it in a therapeutic setting. I think it's helpful to make the delineation. Thinking about these medicines in a recreational-versus-therapeutic setting is like comparing apples to airplanes."

Alex: "Yeah, I think I get it. I knew people in college who used Ecstasy a lot. But I only used it once. I didn't like how I felt afterwards, and I had no problem never doing it again."

Dr. Dan: "For the pure science of the addiction potential, I like to look at rats, one of our closest mammal relatives. They don't get addicted to MDMA. They don't get addicted to psilocybin. But they can get addicted to cocaine, alcohol, and nicotine."

Alex: "Is it going to make me physically sick?"

Dr. Dan: "MDMA seldom makes people sick. If they do get sick, it's usually because their body was storing a deep experience of trauma that started waking up. But the number of people who get nausea and vomiting is less than 5 percent."

Alex: "How exactly does the whole therapy work?"

Dr. Dan: "Assuming you decide to do this treatment, it's three sessions, spaced over six months, approximately one every two months. Between these medicine sessions, there are some integration therapy sessions as well.

"Before the first medicine session, we get to know each other, talk about why you want to do this, what you hope to get out of the session, and what you think might come up.

"For the first medicine session itself, you'll come here in the morning, around 8:30 a.m., in a fasted state. We'll give you a few medicines to help you relax, primarily a compound called GABA. It helps relax the nervous system into an easy and receptive state. If we just launch somebody with a full dose of MDMA straightaway, the nervous system can be a little jittery, which makes it hard to fully surrender. About an hour later, you'll take the first dose of the MDMA.

"There'll be two therapists in the room with you, me and a woman. We always use a man and a woman, both for practical and therapeutic purposes.

"It can take anywhere from thirty to sixty minutes for you to feel the effects. For the first hour after taking the MDMA, I'll encourage you to put on your eyeshade, lay back on the sofa, and listen to the music while the medicine takes effect.

"At around an hour, I'll tap you on the ankle and see how your process is going.

"Then, if you'd like it, you can take the second booster dose. That is optional, though most people take it.

"At that point—when you take the second dose—you'll be in the experience, and you might want to talk about it. If you need to talk, we can talk. If not, that's okay too.

"My job is to be supportive and to help you continue to move through the process. If it feels like you're getting a little bogged down in some of the details or it's too overwhelming, I might guide you through that process.

"You might just be in the midst of an expanded feeling state, and there may not be a whole lot of words. You might just want to lay there and get in touch with how your body's responding to what's coming up.

"We'll do that for a period of time. Then I'll invite you to go back under the eye mask, get connected with the music, get connected with your breath, and reconnect with the process.

"Usually, the experience lasts about four to five hours.

"As you start to come down, we'll talk more about what you experienced. After about six to eight hours, we'll be done. Does that all make sense?"

Alex: "So, what if I change my mind halfway through? Is there an off switch? Or am I just along for the ride?"

Dr. Dan: "There's no real clear antidote. When you're in, you're usually in.

"But that being said, I like to say the best thing about MDMA is that it's always your friend. The medicine is very gentle, and you can, to some extent, modulate its impact. It's much easier to modulate than a true psychedelic, like psilocybin or LSD.

"In my experience, if you just take off your eye mask and sit up, the intensity of the medicine can go down substantially. Often the intensity goes down 80 or 90 percent, depending on the person. That's usually enough to get back to a stable place."

Alex: "You're telling me that if this gets to be too much, just taking the eyeshade off and sitting up makes me okay?"

Dr. Dan: "Yeah, the vast majority of the time. And if things are really intense, and you're in the midst of a massive freak-out, then yes, there is a pharmaceutical that we can use. A benzodiazepine, like Xanax."

Alex: "Does this happen a lot? Do people need sedatives on MDMA?"

Dr. Dan: "I've heard of it, yes, but in my experience, it's never happened."

Alex: "Why do I wear an eyeshade?"

Dr. Dan: "A couple reasons: The first is that sight takes up a large portion of your cognitive resources. By cutting off your visual senses, it forces the brain to focus on other senses, especially the sense of feeling. This enables you to get more impact from the medicine. Wearing an eye mask helps you go deeper and get more connected with yourself. Does that make sense?"

Alex: "Yep."

Dr. Dan: "The other main reason is that, in our experience, we find that people who do not wear masks during this treatment tend to be far more distracted and get less out of the therapy. If you want to take your eye mask off during conversation, you can, of course."

Alex: "I get it. That's why people close their eyes when they meditate."

Dr. Dan: "Exactly right; great insight. People have been meditating for thousands of years, and to be honest, we borrowed many of the processes and rituals for this therapy from other established traditions. Even though MDMA is a relatively new and man-made substance, there is deep wisdom from many cultures around emotional healing, and we try to use that knowledge with these more modern compounds."

Alex: "Why do you play music during the session?"

Dr. Dan: "We've found that music, like eyeshades, helps take the focus off your rational thinking mind and put it more into your emotional, feeling mind. It helps you get out of your head and into your body, so to speak. We design the music very specifically to help you both relax and go deeper."

Alex: "Is this going to change my personality? Or am I still going to be the same person?"

Dr. Dan: "Yes, you'll absolutely be the same person. During the whole experience, you will be in your right mind. You'll know who you are, where you are; you'll know what time it is—all of that.

"This isn't a psychedelic where the experience can be very boundary-shattering. On MDMA, most everyone is very aware of everything around them.

"You're going to be a more enhanced, integrated version of yourself, while still the same person. You're going to still have all the same quirks and uniqueness, but you're going to be more in touch with who you are.

"If anything, you're a fuller, more authentic version of yourself. This is because, oftentimes, through programming or trauma, we've stopped doing and being who we really are. All of those parts of ourselves that we have been cut off from usually come back home."

Alex: "How do I know this is gonna actually work?"

Dr. Dan: "You don't. I can't predict that. And you can't predict that."

Alex: "So, it could have no effect?"

Dr. Dan: "I've heard of cases where it seemed to have no impact on people. In my experience, that has never happened. There's always some effect. And if we look at the numbers, the vast majority of people that go through this experience have massive benefits.

"If I was to bet it against any other single technology, in its effectiveness and its efficacy, there's nothing else that holds a candle. So, if I was to bet, I would bet you'd have a pretty transformative process."

Alex: "I'm in talk therapy; will this interfere with that?"

Dr. Dan: "First off, it's great you're already in therapy. My experience is that this work enhances therapy. We highly recommend people only do this work while in some form of therapeutic practice.

"What therapy does is help reestablish a trusting bond with somebody who cares about your wellbeing and is able to provide a safe container for you to start exploring yourself emotionally and mentally. This medicine enhances that. Does that track with your therapeutic experience?"

Alex: "Yeah, pretty much."

Dr. Dan: "It's a great synergistic tool with talk therapy, and people who already have a therapist tend to have better integration support and get more out of the medicine.

"The only time I've seen it go not so well is when a therapist had a judgment against these tools and didn't want clients to use them. That can be a bit of a conflict."

Alex: "Do I have to talk to my therapist about this ahead of time?"

Dr. Dan: "Ideally, yes. It's helpful to be transparent with the therapist just so that you don't feel like you have to hold something back from that trusted relationship.

"If your therapist isn't open to it, then you might ask them what their thoughts are on this kind of work? Have they explored it? Have they seen the science? Have they read any books or studies or watched documentaries?

"MDMA has only recently been legalized. It went through extensive clinical trials all over the world to be green-lighted by the FDA and DEA as a breakthrough therapy because the clinical data was, quite frankly, incredible. For example, in one early study, more than 80 percent of people with treatment-resistant and chronic PTSD were literally cured from two or three sessions of MDMA. They no longer meet criteria for the clinical diagnosis of PTSD, which many people thought was impossible. This is an astounding result.

"But there are still many therapists who don't know about it or understand it. So, if your therapist does not understand, I'm happy to talk to them, of course."

Alex: "What about my family? Do I have to tell them I'm doing this?"

Dr. Dan: "You don't have to do anything. Ideally, this is a shared, supportive choice with you and people closest to you. Are you in a committed relationship with anyone?"

I laughed.

Alex: "Not really. I'm pretty single. Unless you count my dog, but we aren't really dating."

Dr. Dan: "Okay, well, if you had a primary human partner and you'd been in a long-term relationship, especially if you live together, it's usually better for that person to know and to support you."

Alex: "I don't have that, but I do have my family, who I'm pretty close to, I guess, but I don't live with them or anything."

Dr. Dan: "Then, I think it's your choice."

Alex: "What if I tell them, and they're not on board?"

Dr. Dan: "It can be complicated. If they're against a safe, legal therapy, they may be projecting their prejudices and biases onto your experience.

"So, if you get the sense they're not going to approve, but you're pretty sure that this is a path you want to take, you might be better off not telling them straight out of the gate. But again, this is your choice."

Alex: "What could go wrong? What's the worst-case scenario?"

Dr. Dan: "The medical issues we discussed would be the worst-case scenario. But, of course, that wouldn't happen if you've been honest about your medical history. In this situation, the worst-case scenario is you are not able to trust your own experience."

Alex: "What does that mean?"

Dr. Dan: "The number-one handicap to this work is expectation. When somebody comes in with an expectation, and they don't get what they thought they were supposed to get, they might deny what they received. They'll let the treasure go because it wasn't what they thought it would be. A patient I had once described it to me with this metaphor:

"He thought he was going to come in and get a red Ferrari.

"But the medicine gave him a helicopter.

"He said he didn't want the helicopter; he saw a picture of a red Ferrari and wanted that.

"And the medicine told him that helicopters could fly.

"He said that's not what he wanted; he wanted the Ferrari.

"And the medicine tried again to tell him that he'd have to actually go places that you couldn't go to if you were on the ground in a Ferrari.

"But he was so insistent on the Ferrari that he turned down the helicopter.

"He said he realized the gifts he'd missed later, and on his second session, he surrendered to the gifts that came, and that session was great.

"The best way to avoid this mistake is to come in with an open heart and surrender to what comes up."

Dr. Dan was nothing like any doctor I'd ever talked to. He was like if Mr. Rogers was crossed with Dr. Oz.

This whole thing sounds pretty great. Can it be this good and this easy?

CHAPTER 2

Dr. Dan Questions Alex

Alex: "If I decide to do it, what are the next steps?"

Dr. Dan: "The next step is for me to ask you some questions."

Alex: "Weren't those all answered on the intake form I filled out?"

Dr. Dan: "That was the initial intake screening. It covered your basic medical and health issues to make sure you're even eligible for the treatment.

"I'd like to know you better and to ensure you know what to expect from the therapy. This therapy is amazing for the right people, but it's not right for everyone. If we choose to move forward together, I'd like to make sure everyone has very clear expectations.

"Are you okay with me asking you some questions? I don't have to. Again, you get to choose if and how you move forward."

I nodded.

Dr. Dan: "What made you interested in this work?"

Alex: "My friend Anne—who you treated—did it. I talked to her about it a lot, and it seemed pretty appealing, so I thought I'd try it. I've also read a little bit about this. And I've seen other people I follow on social media talk about it too."

Dr. Dan: "What change did you see in Anne or these other people that appealed to you?"

Alex: "So much has changed for her. She used to be in the same role as me at work, and now she's in charge of a whole department.

"She got engaged to the guy she had been dating forever, and they now have wedding plans. I'm not looking to get married, but still, it was cool to see that. They do so much cool stuff that she never used to do before, like painting class or weekend trips to fun places.

"And she lost twenty pounds in a year, without some crazy diet where she only ate meat or only drank celery juice or anything ridiculous like that.

"She also stopped drinking. Not totally. She'll still have a beer or two at happy hour, but that's it.

"I mean, she's the same person, just better."

Dr. Dan: "That sounds like an incredible change. Tell me more."

Alex: "You know what's funny? Her desk used to be right next to mine, and we used to wallow in our misery together, I guess you could say. We'd send each other funny memes about being depressed or not feeling our emotions or making fun of people—stuff like that."

Dr. Dan: "And now?"

Alex: "We still get along great, but she's always in such a good mood, and she doesn't really engage on that level anymore. She was never mean about it...she kind of moved on. We don't even hang out much anymore—mainly, because she got promoted and has so much going on in her life. I was depressed about it at first, but then I realized—I wanted that too."

Dr. Dan: "I'm glad to hear this therapy helped her so much. So, tell me—what are you hoping to get out of this therapy for yourself?"

Alex: "I guess I want to feel better. To get more out of my life."

Dr. Dan: "Say more about that."

Alex: "Dr. Dan, I feel like I've always done everything I was supposed to do. I went to college; I got a decent job; I'm doing well at it. But...I feel like my life isn't what I want it to be.

"I don't know if this is the solution, but I do know the results I've seen in Anne, and I want that in my life. I want to be a better me, I guess."

Dr. Dan: "Is that all?"

Alex: "I'm willing to work hard. I feel like I've tried everything I can. I've tried yoga, I've tried meditation, I've tried talk therapy,

I've tried CrossFit, I've tried veganism, I've tried making more money, I've tried sex, I've tried drugs, and I've tried music. I've tried everything I can to chase away my sadness…but nothing has worked. Nothing helped me get the life I want to have.

"Honestly, if I really think about it…I'm lost and I'm lonely and I'm sad, and I don't know what to do about it."

Dr. Dan: "What kinds of things do you currently do to feel better?"

Alex: "What do you mean?"

Dr. Dan: "For example, you tried yoga, meditation, things like you said, but they didn't work. So, what else are you trying right now?"

Alex: "Like I told you, I've had a therapist I've been going to for about a year. I like her a lot; she's helped some. I started going because Anne recommended it, actually."

Dr. Dan: "That's great. How often do you see her?"

Alex: "Once a week."

Dr. Dan: "Okay, if you decide you want to do this, we're going to have to talk about some changes that may need to happen beforehand. Going to talk therapy once a week is great, but for many people, that may not be enough integration work."

Alex: "Why not?"

Dr. Dan: "MDMA-assisted psychotherapy can be very rough

for many people. I'm not saying this to scare you, but I like to set very clear expectations. Listen to what I'm about to tell you:

"When you begin MDMA therapy, things may get harder before they get easier.

"And that can be scary at times. Yes, the medicine is your friend, but it can bring up some challenging emotions and realizations.

"You will almost certainly realize some hard truths. They may or may not be welcome to you, but they will most definitely be challenging to you. In some rare cases, for people with severe PTSD in their past, sometimes hidden or forgotten traumas come up. I've seen that happen many times.

"Because of what you learn about yourself, or what memories or emotions come up, you may end up changing your entire life.

"I like to make sure everyone who goes through this has a solid integration practice and support system for themselves."

Alex: "So, you're saying this could mess up my life?"

Dr. Dan: "No, definitely not. It will almost certainly change your life. But in what ways it changes your life, I cannot be sure.

"For example, if you work in a super driven industry and trauma comes up during the session, it's not always the most convenient thing to work through. Sometimes trauma can be disruptive to your work or career, at least for a period.

"It can be disruptive to your relationships too, especially if your partner or family doesn't know what you're doing or is not onboard and understanding.

"And depending on the dynamic in your family—I don't want to necessarily use the word 'co-dependent,' but—if trauma comes up into the space, those relationships can be affected.

"One of the benefits of these medicines is that they are disruptive to our psyche. That's how it helps us grow. But because they're disruptive, they can be uncomfortable."

Alex: "Is this going to be painful?"

Dr. Dan: "Describe what you mean by 'painful.'"

Alex: "I'm not sure. I'm not so worried about the physical stuff. Emotional pain, I guess."

Dr. Dan: "I appreciate you getting in touch with that question and being able to voice it. Because, oftentimes, just in voicing the fear, we start to get more ownership of it.

"To answer your question: yes, if you get in touch with something that's emotionally uncomfortable, it can be painful.

"But again, discomfort is kind of the point of this therapy. The only way to get hard emotions out is to let them come up. Not all of it will be hard, but the hard parts are how you heal. When you do this therapy, you're creating the space for any trauma you have to resurface, so that you can integrate it and let it go."

Alex: "So, this can bring up a lot of deep trauma, right? And it'd be hard and painful for me?"

Dr. Dan: "That's the hardest part of this kind of work, yes. If there is any deep and painful trauma, this therapy will often bring it up.

"But the reason that this medicine is so amazing for PTSD—and it's the single best agent we know of for post-traumatic stress—is because it brings us into open-hearted space in order to get in touch with our deeper pain.

"What might be too hard to handle normally becomes less over-whelming. You can imagine it like being tackled but with lots of padding on. You'll feel the impact, but it doesn't register as pain because there is so much cushion around you."

Alex: "Hold on. You keep talking about PTSD, but I don't have that. I kind of just want to feel better. So, is this right for me?"

Dr. Dan: "Classically, in psychiatry, we've identified PTSD as being a very bad event that occurred in a person's life where they thought they were going to die. And that trauma gets 'stuck' in them, to the point where they still have flashbacks and night-mares and a re-experiencing of that original trauma. We used to think this was just with major events like war and rape; we called this 'acute trauma.'

"What we know now is that there's actually a much larger land-scape of trauma. There's something called complex trauma, which is a more and less acute process, but just as impactful for someone.

"There's also attachment trauma, which involves someone not having secure attachments, which can be very traumatizing for a person, especially children.

"For example, maybe your parents didn't give you the love that you wanted or needed. Maybe you got picked on at school a lot. Maybe a bully was harassing you, so you had to find a new way to keep yourself safe.

"Maybe there was something that your parents experienced in their childhood, meaning were going through their own trauma and then projected it onto you. They might have unintentionally taught you to believe the world's not a safe place, that you can't trust love, that people will screw you if you give them the chance.

"All of those things are all mental programs that can be considered trauma. Trauma is not only this classic kind of war-related 'soldiers in the battlefield' PTSD. All of these traumas are relevant and important to our lives, and if we have trauma like this in our lives, it's usually holding us back, and this therapy can help."

My head was spinning, and I wasn't entirely sure I could explain why. I felt almost angry, and even combative, which didn't make sense.

Alex: "Are you telling me that my parents not loving me is the same as going to war or being raped? That doesn't sound right at all to me."

Dr. Dan: "No, not at all. It's not the same thing, but it is on the same spectrum. Everything is on a spectrum, right?

"I can shoot free throws, but I'm never going to be Michael Jordan.

"I can write a poem, but I'm never going to be Emily Dickinson.

"I've had depression, but I've never committed suicide. I've thought about suicide, and I had bad depression for a time. And my sister committed suicide. So, did we have the same kind of depression?

"All of our mental landscapes and our emotional landscapes are on a spectrum. If somebody has gone to war, and they've seen death and almost got killed, I think there's a high likelihood that they have the classic form of PTSD.

"If we didn't get the love that we wanted as children—or we lived in some kind of childhood experience where we didn't feel safe—where it wasn't safe for us to be who we were—we didn't feel totally safe with those that were caring for us, then we're also on the trauma spectrum…just not at the same point as someone who has seen death in war. Does that make sense?"

Alex: "Yeah, I think so. It just seems weird to compare my parents to war."

Dr. Dan: "I'm not judging or comparing your parents to anything. It's just a recognition that, yeah, life is really unpredictable, and we may not have been loved just the way we wanted or had the security just the way we wanted it. And yes, not having our needs met as a child can be a trauma that still impacts us."

Alex: "So, I can have trauma, even if I didn't have that bad of a life?"

Dr. Dan: "Broadly speaking, yes. But what do you mean by 'that bad of a life'?"

Alex: "One of the things that I battle with is that I feel like I didn't have that bad of a life. My parents weren't perfect, but they weren't that bad. No one beat me or sexually abused me or anything.

"I wonder if I deserve to do this sort of therapy. I mean, shouldn't it only be for people who actually went through hard stuff? Like rape victims or people who suffered through severe hardship, like oppression or war? That wasn't me."

Dr. Dan: "I believe every person deserves the opportunity to deal with their problems. Just because you didn't have the hardest life possible, doesn't mean you don't deserve to heal whatever pain you have.

"We all have a need to be safe and secure. We have a need to experience our own power and serve through that power. We have a need to love and feel loved. We have a need to express ourselves. We have a need to grow and become more intelligent and wiser over time.

"If those needs are not met, they'll come out sideways as some kind of external violence, or it will get internalized in some way, like anxiety and depression."

I was struggling to follow Dr. Dan's explanation. I didn't disagree with him. I almost felt like I wasn't even hearing him, like my mind could not process his words and was pushing me away.

This seems so strange to me. I was paying attention and totally into the conversation not even ten minutes ago, but now it was like my mind was going blank.

Alex: "You talked about this a while ago—how MDMA therapy

can interfere with your life. That's the thing that I keep coming back to, and I don't know if I should worry more about this."

Dr. Dan: "We all have patterns of avoiding certain things. We avoid things that're uncomfortable, or we don't want to look at. Those avoidance patterns can be anything that keeps emotional discomfort at bay—for example: drugs, alcohol, overeating, self-sabotage, avoiding vulnerability, intimacy in relationships, social media, playing video games, or anything else that we will use to anesthetize or try and numb out emotional pain.

"Even very successful people do this. In fact, many successful people will become successful precisely because they're avoiding the experience of looking at their own feelings of low self-worth or internal inadequacy. Success and overwork are how they avoid these feelings.

"So, if you have any avoidance patterns and you do this work and get in touch with the feelings you are avoiding, that can be hard. This work can challenge those old avoidant behavioral patterns because now the underlying emotions are coming to the surface."

Alex: "Can you explain this a little more?"

Dr. Dan: "Sure. I'll use my life as an example: A big reason I became a doctor is because I had my own unresolved trauma. My trauma was very painful, and I avoided it by focusing so much time and effort on school and achievement. Unconsciously, I thought the social and material success of being a doctor would fill the void and make me feel worthy.

"It did not.

"This ended up making me more traumatized and depressed and isolated because, after I became a doctor, my life didn't really change—except that now I had a hard job and no goals to work towards anymore. In order to resolve the issue, I had to do my trauma work. And I did. And I continue to do it."

Alex: "You're saying this could really hurt and ruin my life and my relationships with my family?"

Dr. Dan: "From a certain perspective, that's possible. But in the long run, it can help them become better."

Alex: "Or ruin them, right? Isn't that what you meant?"

Dr. Dan: "Yes. It can help people see and potentially end dysfunctional relationships.

"If everybody's involved and willing to do the work, then I've seen it go into a healing arc. That's why it's helpful for the people around you to know that you're doing this work with trusted people and that they're willing to support you. It's also important that they be willing to look at their own stuff.

"If the person who you are in an abusive relationship with is not willing to look at the level of pain that you've been feeling, then yes, it can alter that relationship so that it's no longer the relationship you've known."

Alex: "That's ruining the relationship."

Dr. Dan: "I wouldn't describe that as ruining the relationship. This therapy can transition the relationship. And I have seen that happen. For example, if someone is in relationship with an abusive partner and they get in touch with their own power to say, 'This is no longer okay'—unless the partner is willing to do their own work, that relationship can transition and could end."

Alex: "So, basically, ending relationships: that's how it can be disruptive."

Dr. Dan: "Dysfunctional relationships, but yes, it can end them.

"Alex, this medicine and this work will almost certainly change your life. It's not always easy, and at the beginning, it can be very disruptive. This is not something to come into lightly. Like I told you: things can get harder before they get easier. If you choose to do this, do it knowing that the road ahead can be very challenging at times."

My head was spinning. It felt like too much to take in. I'd never felt this confused and almost—I don't know another word for it—blank.

Alex: "Dr. Dan, I'm not sure what to do. What do you think I should do?"

Dr. Dan: "I can't make that decision for you. I can tell you that you don't have to make your decision now. We can keep talking about it. It's never too late. I've known people in their mid-sixties and -seventies who've worked with these medicines and had transformational experiences with them.

"When everything has been discussed and taken into consideration, I have not seen it go poorly or have a bad outcome. Occasionally, it will be uncomfortable for reasons that we've already mentioned, but everyone I've worked with who did their work is always very glad they did it.

"But I'm happy to stay in the conversation with you because I do believe that once you have the majority of your questions answered, you'll find your own truth and your own way."

My mind was frozen. Totally blank. I didn't know what to say, so I was pretty shocked by the next statement to come out of my mouth.

Alex: "I don't think I want to do this. I'm sorry."

Dr. Dan: "This is perfectly fine. This is the best decision for you now, and I'm glad you're in touch with your truth.

"I've never once tried to persuade or convince someone to do this. Everyone has to come to this work in their own way, in their own time.

"If you ever want to talk about doing it, I'm here. Until then, good luck, and I will be rooting for you."

I got to my feet and slowly walked out the door. I'm not even sure I said goodbye to Dr Dan.

CHAPTER 3

"What Happened?"

I got into my car, sweaty and anxious.

What the hell just happened?

For the first part of my conversation with Dr. Dan, I'd assumed I was going to do it.

I had no idea what changed. Or when the discomfort started. I can't even understand why I didn't want to do it.

I wasn't angry at Dr. Dan. Or even at myself. I couldn't figure it out.

Where is this gut-level aversion coming from? I thought about how great it had sounded, or how cool Dr. Dan was, or how amazing Anne had been after her therapy.

But I couldn't make myself walk back in there and say, "Yes."

I went back to work, where I ran into Anne in the break room later that day.

Anne: "Alex! I haven't seen you in a while. You been avoiding me?"

Alex: "I've been trying to, but you keep creeping on me like this. Don't you have a boyfriend?"

We laughed. MDMA therapy or not, Anne still had a great sense of humor.

Anne: "How was your meeting with Dr. Dan?"

Alex: "Pretty good. He's such a nice guy. Not like any doctor I've ever met. He listened to me and told me about his life. I liked him a lot."

Anne: "I know, right? Isn't he great? So, when is your session?"

Alex "I don't know…I don't think I'm going to do it."

She kinda stopped and looked confused. Then, she shrugged her shoulders.

Anne: "Oh. Okay. Well, if it's not right for you, then that's okay too."

Weirdly, I was kinda disappointed that Anne didn't try to talk me into it.

CHAPTER 4

Alex Returns to Real Life

Two days later, I went to see my therapist, Dr. Kate, and told her the whole story.

Alex: "So, what do you think?"

Dr. Kate: "What do *you* think?"

This was the game we'd play. I'd ask her what she thought, and then she'd turn it back on me. I used to be so frustrated with that, but this time, it was almost funny.

Alex: "Oh come on! I'm really confused. At least tell me what you think."

Dr. Kate: "Okay, be more specific: what do I think about *what*?"

Alex: "I don't know, the whole thing. Am I crazy?"

Dr. Kate: "I don't think so."

Alex: "Why didn't I do it?"

Dr. Kate: "Why do *you* think you didn't do it?"

Alex: "I don't know!"

Kate: "If you did know, what would the answer be. Just hypothetically?"

Alex: "I guess…I'm afraid."

Dr. Kate: "Why might you be afraid?"

Alex: "I'm just afraid, and I can't figure out why."

Dr. Kate: "That's understandable. This sort of therapy can be scary. It can bring on serious changes, and changes can be frightening."

Alex: "Yeah, but it's safe."

Dr. Kate: "I know."

Alex: "I mean, it's like one of the safest medicines you can take."

Dr. Kate: "Yes, it is."

Alex: "And it really works. It totally changes people's lives."

Dr. Kate: "I know."

Alex: "And it's supposed to be so freeing. You, like, face all your stuff but feel safe doing it."

Dr. Kate: "Oh yes, I know."

Something about the way she responded to that gave me pause. There was something behind her statement I'd never heard from her.

Alex: "Let me ask you something: what do you think of MDMA therapy? I've never even asked you that."

Dr. Kate: "What do I think of it? I think it's amazing."

Alex: "Can I ask you a personal question?"

Dr. Kate: "It depends on the question."

Alex: "Have you done MDMA therapy?"

Dr. Kate stared at me for a long time, not saying anything. I started to get fidgety and anxious.

Alex: "Did I say something wrong?"

Dr. Kate: "Not at all. I'm just not sure how to answer that."

Alex" "It's a yes-or-no question. Those are usually the easiest to answer."

I laughed, but Dr. Kate didn't.

Dr. Kate: "It's not that simple for me. I don't want to lie to you, but I also don't want to create undue influence on you. It's important for you to make your own decision about this."

Oh my god!

Alex: "You've done MDMA therapy!"

Dr. Kate: "Yes."

Alex: "Why didn't you tell me before? I want to know what it's like, how it affected you—everything!"

Dr. Kate sighed and shifted in her chair.

Dr. Kate: "This is why I was hesitant to talk about it."

Alex: "You had a bad experience?"

Dr. Kate: "Quite the opposite. But I don't want me or my experience to be the basis for your decision, one way or the other."

Alex: "Oh come on, Dr. Kate! If you won't tell me about your experience, at least tell me what you think about MDMA overall."

Dr. Kate: "In my professional opinion, MDMA is an incredible medicine and one of the best things that's ever happened to talk therapy."

I was *not* expecting her to say that. I didn't know why, but I honestly thought she might be against taking something that wasn't legal until only a few years ago.

Alex: "Why?"

Dr. Kate: "Talk therapy is great, but most people never get past the intellectual side of it. They never actually get past the words and into feeling their feelings. In my experience, MDMA helps people do exactly that: it facilitates the ultimate goal of talk therapy, which is healing trauma."

Alex: "You've had patients who've done it?"

Dr. Kate: "Yes."

Alex: "What was their experience like?"

Dr. Kate: "For most of them, it was a transformative experience that helped them push past blocks that years of just talking did not. Many of them said it was the best experience of their life."

I was gob-smacked. This was just about the opposite thing I would've expected from her.

I mean, I liked her because she didn't put up with BS and called me on it, but that same part of her just made me assume she'd think MDMA was "cheating" or something like that.

I realized I hadn't actually thought it through because she was always so open and non-judgmental.

Alex: "Your patients are glad they did it?"

Dr. Kate: "Oh yes. Each of the ones I've had who did it."

Alex: "So, you think I should do it?"

Dr. Kate: "I'm not saying that at all."

Alex: "You just said it was the greatest thing ever."

Dr. Kate: "For the people who choose to do it, yes, they said that. But it's not good for everyone."

Alex: "What do you mean?"

Dr. Kate: "This is serious medicine. How you come to it is very important. In many ways, the choice to do it is part of the therapeutic process itself. Did you notice how Dr. Dan first answered your questions and then started asking you questions?"

Alex: "Yeah."

Dr. Kate: "He was assessing your readiness for the medicine. Why you came to it and what you're hoping to accomplish is as important as anything you do with the actual medicine. He was also evaluating you. In some sense, he was making sure you were ready."

Alex: "What do you mean?"

Dr. Kate: "He told you that it can make your life more difficult. Did he also mention that it can bring up lots of uncomfortable memories? That the experience can be very intense and even terrifying?"

Alex: "Yeah. I mean, he didn't use the word 'terrifying,' but he was pretty clear about how things often get harder before they get easier."

Dr. Kate: "Was that when you started to change your mind?"

Alex: "Yeah, I guess it was."

Dr. Kate gave me that look again. Except this time, I wasn't laughing at our little game.

Alex: "Oh man, I get it. He told me the downsides to see how I'd react."

Dr. Kate: "Right."

Alex: "And I failed the test."

Dr. Kate: "No. You're being far too hard on yourself. That wasn't a test. There's no pass or fail. He was doing his job as a physician and facilitator to help you make the right decision *for you*.

"People who come to MDMA therapy casually don't do as well. For this medicine to be effective, you have to be ready to uncover your truth and willing to change because of it."

Alex: "So, I'm not ready?"

Dr. Kate: "Only you can determine that."

Alex: "I honestly don't know if I'm ready."

Dr. Kate: "That's okay."

Alex: "How will I know if I'm ready?"

Dr. Kate: "Why did you consider doing MDMA therapy to begin with?"

Alex: "For the same reasons I'm here, I guess. Because I'm unhappy. Because I want to change. Because I don't know how to have the life I want, and the people who do this therapy seem to have it. Because I'm sick of being stuck."

Dr. Kate: "Do you believe MDMA therapy can help you do all those things—help you change, become happier, get the life you want, get unstuck, etc.?"

Alex: "It worked for my friend Anne. And other people I've read about. The data seems really clear that it works. So, yes, I think it can."

Dr. Kate: "Okay. Then, the question is: do you really want to change?"

Alex: "What do you mean?"

Dr. Kate: "You said you believe MDMA therapy works. My question is simple: *do you really want to change?*"

Alex: "Yeah. I mean, of course. Why not?"

Dr. Kate: "You said, 'No' to the therapy."

I felt myself sweating. Why was I sweating? She wasn't being mean or grilling me. These were simple questions.

Alex: "But I want to change."

Dr. Kate: "Why say, 'No' to the therapy? Now, please understand, I am *not* saying you should or should not do it. I'm just asking about this contradiction."

Alex: "What contradiction?"

Dr. Kate: "You say you want to change, but you turn down a

therapy that you believe will help you make that change. That is a contradiction."

Alex: "It is?"

Dr. Kate: "Maybe there's another way you plan to accomplish the change you say you want. Is there some other thing you're doing instead of MDMA therapy?"

Alex: "No..."

Dr. Kate: "So, you're going back to the exact life you had before. The one you said you were stuck in and didn't like."

Alex: "Yeah..."

Dr. Kate: "The only conclusion from this set of facts is that you don't actually want to change."

Alex: "But I do."

Dr. Kate: "Why don't your actions reflect that? Either the belief is off, or the actions are off because they contradict.

"If you want to change, you'll do something to try to change. If you don't want to change—which is okay—then you won't do something to change. Both are fine, but they're a contradiction. Do you see the contradiction?"

Alex: "Now I do."

Dr. Kate: "I'm not trying to convince you to do the therapy or not. Just trying to help you unpack your thinking."

I didn't know what to say.

Alex: "I feel like I can't even think about this. Like I'm blank."

Dr. Kate: "That's probably your ego."

Alex: "I'm not being arrogant!"

Dr. Kate: "No, no. I mean 'ego' in the psychological definition, not the common definition."

Alex: "What's the difference?"

Dr. Kate: "Let's use a different term for 'ego': your protective self.

"Everyone has a 'protective self' inside of them that has one job: to keep you alive. And it often interprets that goal as keeping you the same. Not letting you change.

"This is why so many people have such a hard time changing: their ego—or protective self, as I call it—is literally designed to prevent them from changing."

Alex: "Seriously?"

Dr. Kate: "Oh yes. Imagine the protective self as the most anxious and overprotective helicopter parent you can imagine. It thinks everything is a danger, and any change means the risk of total destruction."

Alex: "That sounds awful."

Dr. Kate: "No, it has a very important role inside of you. It keeps you alive.

"But yes, it can also hold you back from growth. All of us, in order to grow and expand as people, must understand that we have a protective self, that it's our friend trying to help us, but that it doesn't want us to change. We don't have to listen to it all the time. We can assess the risks and decide change is worth it.

"A big part of therapy is understanding how the ego—or protective self—has overstepped its bounds. For many people, therapy is about realizing how their fear of dying keeps them from growing their life."

I thought about this for a while.

What if I was wrong? What if I wasn't ready?

What if that horrible blank feeling was trying to warn me that I couldn't handle the things that MDMA would bring up?

CHAPTER 5

A Conversation with Pa

The whole next week sucked.

Work sucked.

Life sucked.

Even Netflix sucked. I couldn't find anything I wanted to watch. I just scrolled through the options endlessly and couldn't focus on anything.

I couldn't get Dr. Kate's words out of my head:

"The only conclusion is you don't actually want to change."

At first, I was pissed at her. *How dare she say that?*

Then, I realized she was right.

Then, I got pissed at her for being right.

Then, I got pissed at myself for not facing the fact that she was right.

Then, I got pissed at her again for being right.

Which made me laugh because it was all so ridiculous. I was spinning in circles, with no idea what to do except laugh at myself running in mental circles in my head.

Then, out of nowhere, I got a call from my grandfather.

Alex: "Pa, how are you doing?"

Pa: "Alex, where are you kid?"

Alex: "At home."

Pa: "So, I guess no dinner? You should have at least called. Granny Jane was worried about you."

My heart sunk. I'd been looking forward to this dinner with my grandparents for months. How could I forget about it?

My pa is one of the people I'm closest to. He's always loved me, always backed me, always been there for me. To let him down, to not even call, was like…just what I needed right now to put the cherry on top of the shit-sundae that was my life.

Alex: "Oh no, Pa, I have no idea what happened. Lemme come over now; hold on—"

Pa: "No, no, no. It's too late; it'll take you an hour to get here, and your grandma and I go to bed early."

Alex: "I'm so sorry. Look, tomorrow I can—"

Pa: "Stop apologizing, kid. I'm not mad—I'm worried about you. You sound sad. What happened?"

Alex: "Nothing, everything is fine."

Pa: "You're a terrible liar. You sound like hell. What's going on? You need money? You get dumped?"

Alex: "No, Pa. I'm great. I have a good job, a cool apartment, an awesome dog. What else can I ask for?"

Pa: "Stop bullshitting me, kid. You know I love you, but you also know you can't lie to your Grandpa Bill. Tell me what's going on. The real shit."

How do I even begin to explain this to Pa?

Alex: "I don't even know where to start."

Pa: "Try the beginning, smart guy. That's where stories start: the beginning."

I took a deep breath, sighed, and dove in. I told him the whole story, from start to finish.

One thing about Pa: when you talk, he listens. He listened in complete silence until I was done.

Alex: "I guess all of that was on my mind, and that's why I forgot about dinner. Sorry, Pa."

Pa: "Alex, I want you to listen to me very closely: make your own decision, of course, *but I think you should do it.*"

Alex: "What?"

Pa: "You heard me. Go do it."

Alex: "For real?"

Pa: "Yeah, of course."

Alex: "But…didn't you always tell me not to do drugs?"

Pa: "Of course, I didn't want you to be some coked-out junkie crackhead. But these aren't drugs. This is medical therapy, right? With a doctor? He has his license and what-not?"

Alex: "Yeah, of course, Pa. It's even covered by insurance."

Pa: "Then, go do it."

Alex: "*Really?*"

Pa: "You need it."

Alex: "I *need* it?"

Pa: "Look…kid, you had a rough childhood. Granny and I tried to help you all we could, but I don't think you really understand what your childhood was like. If this will help you, you deserve it."

Alex: "What do you mean? I had a good childhood. I mean,

my parents weren't perfect, but I wasn't beaten or molested or anything."

Pa: "Goddamn right you weren't; I'd kill anyone who did that to you. And yeah, you had a good childhood in a lot of ways, but if we're being honest here, I don't think it was as good as you remember."

Alex: "What? Why?"

Pa: "You were too young to remember, but when you were a little kid, your parents were not around as much as they should have been. It was hard at times."

Alex: "Really?"

Pa: "Oh yeah. They had a real hard time when they were newly married and young, and they separated lots before their divorce. Why do you think you spent so much time with us when you were young?"

Yeah, I was at my grandparents' house a lot. That was partly why I was so close to my pa.

Alex: "I thought you guys wanted me around."

Pa: "I love you more than life itself, but you think I wanted a baby around 24/7? And you cried like the dickens when you were little. Obviously, I loved you, but that was not our choice. Your mother and father had a lot of issues, so Granny and I kept you to try and do our part to help."

Alex: "Wait, what? I didn't know any of this."

Pa: "Well, a lot of it happened when you were real young. There were many nights you cried non-stop because your mom and dad weren't there. Do you not remember that?"

Alex: "I don't know. Not really."

Pa: "I've tried to talk about these issues with your mom for years, but she won't listen to me and then we get to yelling. And to be honest, I get why she's mad. I wasn't always around when she was growing up and wasn't the best parent when I was there. She still hasn't forgiven me for that, and it hurts to say this, but I don't think I've done my part to make up for it. I've always felt guilty about that.

"I don't even think I realized this fully until right now, saying it on the phone to you.

"And honestly, I don't think I realized how much this affected you until now. I mean, I knew, but I don't think I admitted it to myself until you just said it."

Holy shit. I had no idea. This changed everything about me, about my family. I didn't even know how to think about it. My gut was turning over in circles, and I felt that blankness again.

Alex: "Pa…why did you never tell me this?"

Pa: "I don't know, kid. This is hard for me to talk about too. I've had my own issues, and it's not easy to recognize that I wasn't around when they were kids. I spent most of the time they were young working my ass off and providing for the family, and I thought I was doing the right things by them, but looking back, maybe I didn't all the time. I'm getting old now, and I may not have much time left. Remember that heart attack I had six months ago?"

Lord, do I. Pa had a minor heart attack, and I wouldn't leave his bedside. I took a bunch of time off work and stayed with him almost as much as Grandma. It was the hardest time of my life, even though the doctors said he was fine and would fully recover. It really spooked me.

Alex: "Yeah, of course, Pa."

Pa: "Well, that really shook me up. I thought I was done for. Have you noticed how the past few months I've been a lot more open with you? When you come over for dinner, we talk deeper? I hug you more? Stuff like that?"

Alex: "Yeah, of course. It's kinda great. I just thought it was the heart attack."

Pa: "Well, that's part of it. But I'm working through my stuff too. I've even thought about maybe doing some therapy or something like that."

I was speechless. This man was a hard-ass, ex-military, law-and-order, old-school conservative. I mean, he was the definition of a red-state Republican. He called Democrats "commie bastards" and had so many guns that he kept them in a walk-in gun locker!

I *never* imagined he'd be open to this stuff.

Alex: "I had no idea, Pa. You're thinking about therapy?"

Pa: "I considered it, yeah. And I even thought about MDMA."

Alex: "You know about MDMA?"

Pa: "You think I just fell off the turnip truck? Of course, I know about MDMA. I was in the military, and I have friends who saw some real gnarly stuff. That medicine turned their lives around. A few of my friends were in the initial trials that got it legalized."

Alex: "Have you done MDMA?"

Pa: "No. I've talked to a lot of my military friends about their MDMA treatments and other things they've done, and they really opened my eyes. I thought about it, but I've been hesitating."

Alex: "Why?"

Pa: "I'm not sure. It reminds me of the story about the dog and the nail. You know that one?"

Alex: "No. Tell me."

Pa: "There's this old man sitting on his porch, and his old dog is laying next to him. The dog keeps whining like he's in pain. So, I ask the old man, 'Why's your dog whining like that?'"

"He says, 'He's sitting on a big nail. I suppose it hurts him.'

"I ask, 'Why doesn't he move?'

"The old man said, 'I suppose when the pain gets bad enough, he'll move.

"'I guess the pain hasn't been bad enough for me yet.'"

Alex: "Where you'd meet this old guy?"

Pa: "Kid, are you on drugs right now? That's just a damn story to make a point; it didn't actually happen."

We both laughed. Pa and I loved to mess with each other. I knew it was just a story, but I said that anyway, kidding with him.

Alex: "So, you've really thought about doing it?"

Pa: "Yeah, I guess I have. Some. I bet I know why you're hesitating too—you're scared of what's going to come up. If I'm being honest with myself, that's why I'm scared of it too. I told myself I wasn't doing it because I was too old, and I had heart issues.

"But honestly, I think I'm bullshitting myself. I mean, the heart issues are real, but the other stuff—maybe that's an excuse."

This mountain of a man, this paragon of strength that my whole family has relied on for our whole lives...just told me he was afraid of something. I didn't know what to say. He has *never* said that.

Alex: "Pa, I've never heard you talk like this."

Pa: "An old friend passed last week, a guy I was real close to in Vietnam. I had a conversation with him about something related to this just a few weeks before. I'll tell you more about it another time—it really tore me up, though. It's made me think I've got some changes I need to make."

Alex: "Wow, Pa. I had no idea."

Pa: "Yeah, I've been reading about MDMA too. The studies are pretty amazing. You seen those results?"

Alex: "Yeah, I saw."

Pa: "Son, I get why you're afraid. That's just your fear fucking with you. Fuck with it right back. Go take that stuff, and deal with your problems."

Alex: "You really think so?"

Pa: "Kid, you deserve to be happy, and if this can help, how can you say, 'No'?"

Alex: "When you put it like that, I guess you're right."

Pa: "Of course, I'm right; I'm your pa. And I want to hear all about it when you're done—at a dinner you actually attend. You got it?"

Alex: "Deal."

Pa: "Maybe I'll do it too, if it goes well for you. Love you, kid."

That was one thing he always told me, no matter how what—that he loved me.

Alex: "Love you too, Pa."

Through tears, I went to my computer and sent an email to Dr. Dan:

Can we talk again? I changed my mind. I think I want to do it.

CHAPTER 6

Alex Changes His Mind

Dr. Dan greeted me at the door to his office, smiling and offering a warm handshake.

I don't know why, but I half expected him to be cold to me. I guess some part of me thought he would judge me for not wanting to do the therapy.

Dr. Dan: "What prompted you to change your mind?"

Alex: "I talked to my therapist, and she was pretty convincing."

Dr. Dan: "What did she say about it?"

Alex: "She said, *'The only conclusion is you don't actually want to change.'*"

He laughed out loud.

Dr. Dan: "Wow! She said that?"

I recounted the whole conversation and explained my contradiction in detail. It was weird to me how precisely I remembered the conversation, even though I was so confused during the session.

Dr. Dan: "She brings up an excellent point. What do you think about it?"

Alex: "Honestly, man, I think she's right."

Dr. Dan: "Change is hard. I fought change for a long time."

I also told Dr. Dan about my conversations with Anne and my pa. He listened intently, nodding and taking it all in, never once interrupting me. I didn't know what med school he went to, but I'd never seen a doctor who listened like him. He listened like he actually cared.

Dr. Dan: "Okay, let's talk about a few things before you finalize your decision. What's your integration practice? I know you're in talk therapy, but what else do you do?"

Alex: "I have to be honest: I kinda don't know what integration is."

Dr. Dan: "Integration is the method you use to help you take the experience of your MDMA session and make sure you apply lessons to your life.

"The medicine helps you open up, but you still have to actually do the emotional work. 'Integration' is the term we use for the work you do with everything that comes up for you while on the medicine.

"For example, you're in talk therapy, and that's a great integration practice. You'll also talk to me a few times between each session, which is a very important part of integration. We'll discuss what comes up for you, what it means, how to handle it, and what this means for your life.

"You also want to review the notes of what was captured during the MDMA session to make sense of it and unpack it for yourself.

"Other integration practices I recommend are things like creating a flotation practice or a meditation practice. There are so many things you can do; it depends on what works with you."

Alex: "Flotation? Those things in spas where you lay in a salt-water bath?"

Dr. Dan: "Yeah, exactly. It's the first time since conception that a person is without sensory experience. That means your brain isn't tracking as much. There's no sight. It's pitch black. There's no sound. It's totally silent because you have earplugs in. There's no gravity because you're floating in water. There's no need to hold yourself in balance.

"Over 90 percent of what the brain's usually filtering as sensory experience now goes away, so it's easier to see what's in the subconscious. You essentially get to see your mind, so it becomes like meditation on steroids.

"It's also a great way to test out what medicine will be like for you. If you can't hold your stuff together in a float tank, you'll have a hard time holding your stuff together in a medicine journey."

Alex: "Okay, I guess I can do that. Is there anything else I need to do?"

Dr. Dan: "Yes, of course. I'll give you a list as you leave."

Alex: "You've talked a lot about setting the right expectations. Some of the other stuff I've heard about this work says setting the right intention. What's the difference?"

Dr. Dan: "Great question. An intention is what you would like to happen—something you're praying for or really desiring to happen. It's essentially what you are going for.

"An expectation is what you expect to happen. So, for example, your intention in doing MDMA therapy could be to heal. But your expectation might be that, after one session, all your sadness will be gone.

"Does this make sense?"

Alex: "I think so."

Dr. Dan: "To give a more specific example: if you feel really down and sad after your first MDMA session, you might think your intention of being healed is not being met—but that's only because you expected it would happen without pain. But feeling the pain of sadness is often the road to letting it go and healing it.

"I've found the best antidote for expectation is trust and patience. Trust that it's going to happen; patience allows it to arise in its own timing. I like to say that we can't force a flower to open; we can only give it the right conditions for it to happen.

"I like to say: set your intention in motion, have faith that it's going to happen, but let go of your expectation as to how and when it's going to happen, and surrender to what comes up."

Alex: "Okay…I think I get it."

Dr. Dan: "Let me give you one last example. This is a very important point. For me, my biggest prayer coming into medicine work was to open up my heart. I was in a marriage. We were going through a divorce. But I couldn't feel any of it. I was stone cold, and I could see in her how cold I was. Not only could I not feel my stuff, I couldn't even feel her stuff. I was totally shut down. And I knew I didn't want to live the rest of my life like that.

"I made a big prayer. I didn't even know I was making a prayer, but I was like, 'I don't want to live like this the rest of my life.'

"And that was really the only intention I set. I wasn't even praying to anybody, but I was just recognizing that I wanted to find a way to open up my heart.

"And it just happened to be that a few weeks later I was introduced to an underground ayahuasca circle. I learned more about myself in one weekend with ayahuasca than in one decade of psychotherapy. Blasted my heart open.

"I was like, 'Holy shit, this makes everything I just learned in a psychiatry training look like kindergarten.'

"I went back to my wife at the time, and I was like, 'You'll never believe what happened. My heart just got blasted open.'

"Well, she thought I took some drugs and hallucinated. And I was like, 'I'm sorry you feel that way because I'm going to be doing this more.'

"Essentially, I didn't know that in order to live a more open-hearted life, I would have to get in touch with all the trauma that shut my heart down in the first place. And MDMA therapy was a huge part of that journey for me as well.

"So, my intention was to open up my heart. I did get my intention met, and my heart is now far more open than it was. Does that make sense?"

Alex: "Yeah, I get that."

Dr. Dan: "But here's where things got tricky: I had an expectation that opening up my heart was going to be easy. That was clearly not the case. And as that difficulty started to happen, I had to have faith in the process, although it was quite hard.

"My hope was that opening up my heart was going to be a lot easier and take a lot less time. And it didn't happen that way. It took the better part of eight years, and it taught me a lot about being clear with the intention, but I let go of the *how* and the *when*—which are expectations."

Alex: "EIGHT YEARS?!"

He laughed out loud again.

Dr. Dan: "Yes. But the outcome of it has been me living in an open-hearted way and living an open-hearted life in a way that I had never experienced before. And I couldn't have known back then what this was going to feel like. It just took a lot more work and a lot more time than I expected."

Alex: "Man...that sounds really hard."

Dr. Dan: "Yeah, it was. But another lesson I learned that helped me was finding meaning in the suffering.

"Suffering and meaning are inversely proportional. Pain is going to happen. It's inevitable. It is a fact of life. But when my pain has meaning, then there's a lot less suffering."

Alex: "If there was a 'perfect' mindset to come into this work with, what would it be?"

Dr. Dan: "There is no such thing as perfect. Let's say 'optimal' mindset. Here's what someone with the optimal mindset would be like:

"They'd trust the medicine.

"They'd trust their guide.

"They'd trust the process.

"And with all this, they'd then trust their body and mind to heal itself.

"They'd come in with no expectations.

"They'd be willing to surrender to whatever comes up in the sessions.

"They'd receive whatever comes up, be willing to experience it fully.

"And most of all, they'd come to this with the mindset that the medicine is just a tool that helps them do the work. It's not a magic pill that does the work for them."

Alex: "Okay, I think I can do that. I can do my part of the work. I think I'm ready."

Dr. Dan: "Okay, here's the final question I have for you: will you be able to trust the process?"

This question stopped me. I couldn't just say, "Yes," so I sat and thought for a second, and I realized that I didn't actually trust this. Something was off.

Alex: "Dr. Dan, I'm not sure. I mean…I trust you, I guess, but I don't know if I trust the medicine or the process. What am I supposed to trust? Myself? MDMA? How does that work?"

Dr. Dan: "Each of those is separate, but also interconnected.

"First, it's helpful to trust the medicine itself. MDMA is well tested, has been used for a long time, and has a very clear track record of success. Within the parameters we talked about before, it's extremely safe and effective.

"Second, it's helpful to trust the process. MDMA will enable you to bring up and explore some deep emotions, and it will almost certainly be uncomfortable at times. If something is uncomfortable, there's a reason, and it's important for you to experience that. This requires trust that the pain is necessary, that it will end, and that when it does, you'll be in a better place.

"Third, you have to trust me. I'll be there with you in the experience and afterwards, but there may be times when you need more support, and we can talk about how I can give that in the best way possible.

"It's actually essential for you to trust me because you haven't yet built the trust in the medicine yet. That will develop over time. That's why I'm so transparent about my background and my experiences because I believe that the best facilitators have been through their own shit. You can only help people go as far as you've gone."

Alex: "What if it's too much for me to handle?"

Dr. Dan: "This is a common fear: that once you open up, once you start feeling your emotions, you will be overwhelmed by them. Or possibly even die from feeling your emotions. Is that an accurate statement of what you feel?"

I never would have admitted it to myself, but hearing Dr. Dan say it—it felt right.

I'm afraid to feel my feelings.

Alex: "Yeah, that's it. If I feel my emotions, I don't know what'll happen. It might be really bad."

God, even admitting that out loud was both scary and liberating. I felt light-headed and shaky but also exhilarated.

Dr. Dan: "Good, I'm glad you're able to see that fear in yourself. That's a very hard thing for most people to admit. It took me a long time to get there myself.

"So, I commit to being transparent with you, and I commit that I'll do everything I can to help you feel safe and secure as you go through this process.

"Imagine we're going up a new mountain trail. If you were hiking a tall mountain peak, you'd want to go with a guide that knew the path and could prepare you for it. And you would pick a guide because you felt you could trust them to get you there and back safely. I can do that, and you can trust this because I've done it many times.

"But we should only take this journey together if you feel the same way."

Alex: "I do. I feel like I can trust you."

Just saying that, I felt all kinds of…I don't know how to say it. I guess I felt a deep emotional release? It almost made me want to cry.

Dr. Dan: "Good. Then, if you'd like to do the therapy, I'd be happy to facilitate."

Alex: "I'm in."

CHAPTER 7

Learning to Breathe

Dr. Dan: "We have a little bit of time still left in your appointment, so how about we use it to teach you how to breathe?"

Alex: "I'm thirty years old. What've I been doing this whole time?"

Dr. Dan laughed.

Dr. Dan: "That's a common reaction. But just like our society does not teach the most important things in life—how to have a relationship, how to love, how to even do simple things like negotiate a lease—it does not focus on breathing either. There are actually many ways to breathe, and only a few are optimal.

"I'm going to teach you a different way to breathe, a way that can help you regulate your own nervous system. This is an important integration practice that helps you access the experience of safety, presence, centeredness—whenever you choose. Does that make sense?"

Alex: "Honestly, I'm not sure."

Dr. Dan: "Do you understand the sympathetic and parasympathetic nervous systems and how they work?"

Alex: "I kinda remember that from college."

Dr. Dan: "The nervous system is how your body sees, understands, and interprets the world around it, right?"

Alex: "Right."

Dr. Dan: "Generally speaking, the part of your nervous system that is not under your conscious control is divided into two parts: the sympathetic nervous system and the parasympathetic nervous system.

"These systems operate in parallel and control the exact same group of body functions, but they do it in completely opposite ways.

"The sympathetic nervous system prepares the body for high stress or intense physical activity and is often referred to as the 'fight, flight or freeze' response.

"You understand that?"

Alex: "Yeah, I remember 'fight, flight, freeze.' It always reminds me of how people react when you honk at them in traffic.

"Some people get super angry and flip you off or even get out of their car wanting to fight. That's the fight response.

"Some people slam on the gas and speed off. That would be the flight response.

"But most slam on the brakes and look around wildly. That's the freeze response.

"I guess there's also a tiny minority that laugh and wave. I guess those people would be in a parasympathetic state?"

Dr. Dan: "That's not an example I'd ever heard of, but it works great. And as you guessed, the parasympathetic system has almost the exact opposite effect and relaxes the body and inhibits or slows many high-energy functions, which are often referred to as 'rest and digest.'

"Even though in our modern world, no one is in constant danger, most people run around constantly in sympathetic overdrive, meaning they are in a constant 'fight, flight or freeze' response.

"The reasons why are far beyond this conversation, but I believe they come back to a core belief of 'not being enough.' Most people just do not feel like they are enough—good enough, rich enough, smart enough, enlightened enough, etc. This takes a huge toll on both the body and the mind. Does that resonate?"

Alex: "That's why I'm here. I never feel like I'm enough."

Dr. Dan: "These breathing exercises are going to be a very effective way to get you back to a parasympathetic state—a calm, relaxed, 'rest and digest' state."

Alex: "So, you're going to teach me how to relax by breathing?"

Dr. Dan: "Exactly. I'm going to teach you a technique that's been around for thousands of years. It's a variation of what is traditionally called 'pranayama,' otherwise known as the science of breathing.

"Even though it's old, I like to think about it as a new technology. We in the West are only starting to appreciate how well this works, so though it's not new, it is new to us.

"Here's how to do it:

"Step one is breathing from your belly.

"Without going into the deep details, when you're in a sympathetic state—which most people are, most of the time—they breathe in a shallow and rapid way, just in the chest.

"Parasympathetic breath tends to be deeper and wider—meaning less frequent. The breath starts in the belly, then goes up to the chest and into the neck."

Alex: "You mean like a baby, right?"

Dr. Dan: "Exactly right. It's the natural state of parasympathetic breathing.

"Step two is to breathe entirely through your nose, if possible. Both inhale and exhale. If you can't do that, at least inhale through the nose and exhale through the mouth.

"Step three is where we count the time of our inhales and exhales. I like to use a four-count inhale and an eight-count exhale."

Dr. Dan started breathing this way and then counting as he inhaled and exhaled.

Alex: "You want me to literally count as I breathe?"

Dr. Dan: "You can if it's helpful at first, just to get a sense of how to breathe this way. But once you get a sense, it doesn't have to be an exact count."

Alex: "Okay, I can try."

Dr. Dan: "So, let's do this together. Nasal breathing: focus on filling the belly first. We will do the four-count inhale as I bring my hand up, and then the eight-count exhale as I lower my hand."

This really felt weird. I didn't know why, but in all the weirdness surrounding this therapy, practicing breathing together was by far the weirdest thing.

I half expected him to start laughing and tell me he was kidding. But Dr. Dan just closed his eyes and started breathing through his nose. I didn't know what else to do, so I went along.

I didn't know how long we did it, but when Dr. Dan spoke, I realized that I was noticeably relaxed. But it was a different kind of relaxed—like how I usually feel after a massage or something like that.

Dr. Dan: "Somewhere around five to ten minutes is the usual timeframe to really get into a parasympathetic state. How do you feel?"

Alex: "I do feel relaxed. So, this is going to be important...how?"

Dr. Dan: "It's good to build your exit plan before the house is burning down, right? Same thing. It's good to practice feeling like you can lock into a calm, restful state before you're stressed.

"This breathing is an antidote to a panic attack. Instead of breathing about a dozen times a minute, which most people do, you start to breathe, like, four to five times a minute. When you do this over a few minutes, that's known to increase parasympathetic tone, calm you down, and bring you back to a relaxed state.

"Even though these are technologies that are thousands of years old, they are still science-based, proven methodologies that work."

Alex: "So, you're saying I might freak the fuck out. But if I count my breaths properly, I can calm myself down?"

Dr. Dan: "Basically, yes."

I had to admit, I did feel a lot calmer. But I wondered how much weirder this was going to get.

CHAPTER 8

MDMA Therapy Preparation

The rest of the day, I dealt with all the details.

I gave Dr. Dan the contact info for my therapist, so they could connect. He said this is standard practice and wanted to talk to her to make sure they're both on the same page in terms of what they recommend for me.

I set my date two weeks in advance and gave them all my insurance information. Thank god insurance covered most of this because it's many thousands of dollars.

Dr. Dan also introduced me to another woman in his office, Dr. Naomi, who would be co-facilitating my session.

Dr. Dan: "I'll be the primary facilitator, but she'll be there the whole time, just in case she's needed."

We shook hands. She had a great smile and seemed excited to meet me, which was nice.

Alex: "Why two facilitators again?"

I felt terrible as soon as I said it—I didn't mean it as anything bad about Dr. Naomi, but I think it definitely came off the wrong way.

Alex: "I'm sorry; I don't mean anything bad about you. I just was wondering, you know…"

Dr. Naomi: "It's a perfectly fine question. When the FDA legalized this medicine for therapeutic purposes, it did so based on numerous clinical trials that had two facilitators, to ensure the safety of the patient and clinician. That's the standard that was set."

Alex: "Oh…you mean, like, to make sure a patient doesn't get grabby during the session?"

Dr. Naomi: "That's part of it. MDMA is a powerful medicine and some patients can definitely feel a lot of intense feelings, even arousal. While any feeling is appropriate if it comes up, having two facilitators ensures that those feelings stay with the patient and aren't projected onto anyone else."

Alex: "That makes sense. I gotta be honest: I wondered at first if it was something about me that Dr. Dan brought in another person."

We talked a little while longer before Dr. Dan and Dr. Naomi said their goodbyes.

Then Dr. Dan's team ran me through every single detail of what would happen on the day and gave me the document below.

They even made me repeat all their instructions back to them to ensure I understood.

At first, I thought it was kind of ridiculous, but then they explained it to me: many people are very anxious the day they show up, so the less they have to think about logistically, the better.

I have to admit: it helped me feel a lot more confident and relaxed. I probably read the preparation document at least once a day in the weeks leading up to the session.

It was almost like a ritual I developed: every time I got nervous, I'd read it again.

CHAPTER 9

MDMA Therapy Preparation Doc

COMMON QUESTIONS ABOUT MDMA

"How does the medicine work?"

MDMA impacts the major neurotransmitters involved in emotional processing (serotonin, norepinephrine, and dopamine). The release of serotonin heightens positive mood and reduces anxiety, while norepinephrine and dopamine increase energy and alertness.

The medicine increases oxytocin and prolactin levels which are associated with social bonding and love, and it can cause a person to become less receptive to fear inducers and more inclined to social interaction.

The medicine decreases activity in the amygdala, which is the fear center in the brain (overactive in PTSD) and increases activity in the hippocampus (involved in processing memories).

These two effects allow for better recall of all the associated parts of a particular set of memories without as much fear and resistance. The medicine also increases activity in the prefrontal cortex which helps to process and organize information during a state of reduced fear.

Sensations are enhanced and the user experiences heightened feelings of empathy, emotional warmth, self-acceptance, and personal authenticity.

The medicine takes effect thirty to sixty minutes after consumption, with small rushes of exhilaration that can be accompanied by nausea. The effects of the medicine subside after about three to five hours, though if one receives a booster, the effects can last six to eight hours.

Users report that the experience is very pleasant and highly controllable. Even at the peak of the effect, people can usually deal with important matters.

The subjective mental experience feels fairly stable, while creating a dramatic increase in emotional openness and a reduction in fear and anxiety. Unlike most psychedelics, on MDMA, you are always aware of who you are and where you are, and in many cases, people feel even more alert and "sharper" than normal.

People receiving the medicine experience euphoria, positive mood, vigor, and a positively experienced derealization/depersonalization. Users report feeling more talkative and friendly and increased feelings of closeness to others after receiving the medicine.

The medicine, sometimes combined with talk therapy, has shown incredible results in studies, often in just one session. In many cases, there is relief from symptoms that have persisted for years. The medicine has several effects on the brain that appear to make the process of talking through past traumas more effective.

An important principle of an MDMA session is that the healing process is guided by mechanisms from within your own psyche and body. This inner healing intelligence often helps bring conscious attention to difficult feelings, memories, or body sensations, and it allows people to stay present during these challenging experiences rather than avoid or escape from them.

If a particular memory is upsetting or potentially overwhelming, that is a signal your body wants to deal with it. If possible, let it. Remember, we are right here with you. Use your breath and stay with it as much as you can. We know this can be difficult, but we know from experience that this is an important part of the healing. Fully experiencing and expressing this—moving through it instead of away from it—is the way to really heal it.

Ultimately, what MDMA offers is a chance for restoration, to bring everything up that is weighing on your soul, face it, and give yourself permission to heal it and learn from it. This, then, can lead to greater integration into a more mature, stronger experience of self.

The medicine is truly remarkable for working through difficult emotional experiences. When utilized in a safe environment with the intention of personal healing, this tool can help open emotional blockages in the body and heart, increase feelings of emotional safety and connection to others, help shed light on negative self-talk patterns, and help one move into forgiveness towards self and others.

"What are the negative side effects of MDMA?"

First time users of the medicine can experience anxiety, tension, dysphoria, and concern over losing control over the self.

The medicine can increase body temperature, heart rate, and blood pressure, but these effects are temporary.

The medicine may also produce modest changes in immune functioning, lasting up to forty-eight hours.

Other spontaneously reported reactions and common adverse effects include:

- Lack of appetite, insomnia, and muscle tension
- Nausea, dizziness, and tight jaw
- Tooth-grinding, difficulty concentrating, impaired gait and balance
- Dry mouth and thirst, ruminations
- Cold/heat sensitivity
- Paresthesia/tingling
- Anxiety

These effects are transient and diminish as the dose wanes.

"What are the medical exclusions of MDMA?"

There are a few very important medical exclusions of MDMA:

☐ Heart conditions that are affected by increased heart rate and blood pressure. The medicine often increases a person's resting heart rate and can produce an increase in blood pressure.

- Liver problems. While there is little evidence that the medicine causes liver damage on its own, people with hepatitis or other liver ailments may be vulnerable to liver damage if they consume the medicine.
- Seizures. People prone to seizures are more likely to experience them if they take the medicine.
- Psychiatric disorders. The medicine, like many psychoactive drugs, can potentially exacerbate the symptoms of mental illness.
- Malignant hyperthermia. The medicine raises the risk of malignant hyperthermia and heat stroke in people with Central Core Disease.
- Susceptibility to Heatstroke. The medicine increases the risk of heatstroke which is the cause of the vast majority of medicine related fatalities in recreational settings.

"Are there any medicines I can't be on and take MDMA?"

Yes. The medication contraindications are important to note:

- MAOIs
- SSRIs
- Certain antidepressants and many psychotropic medications
- HIV medications
- Medications that are CYP2D6 inhibitors
- Drugs that increase heart rate or blood pressure (many asthma medications; stimulants like cocaine, amphetamine, and caffeine), DXM (Robitussin), stomach acid medications, sedatives (alcohol, opioids, etc.) due to an increased risk of serious adverse effects.

Create your integration practice.

Integration is the work you do before and after the MDMA session to ensure that you get the most out of the medicine. MDMA is not a magic pill and works best as part of a larger program undertaken to do the difficult emotional work. It is hard to put precise percentages on it, but the integration work is almost more impactful than the medicine itself.

The more you have an established integration practice and relationship with at least one good therapist—or some situation where you can really talk with a trusted, wise, supportive friend—the better MDMA will help you.

There are several different ways to create an integration practice. All of these have been used as effective integration practices:

- Talk therapy
- Eating healthy & clean
- Sleeping 8 hours a night
- Working out
- Daily nature walks
- Energy work
- Massage, especially somatic massage
- Acupuncture
- Float sessions
- Sauna/spa
- Epsom salt baths
- Meditation
- Yoga

THE WEEK BEFORE YOUR SESSION

1. Buy these supplements in advance to help your body prepare for and recover from the session.

☐ Melatonin for sleep (if needed)
☐ Magnesium L-threonate for jaw clenching and general relaxation
☐ Vitamin-C for brain health and recovery
☐ Sam-E for after the session, which will help your body restore serotonin levels

2. Set expectations for your family, friends, and colleagues.

You will be totally unavailable for the day of the session. Let people know you'll be out of reach during this time.

3. Arrange transportation to/from the session.

You should *not* drive after your session. Have a friend or family member drive you to and from the location.

4. Avoid alcohol for at least one full day before your session.

Ideally, avoid alcohol for three to five days before (and after) your session if at all possible.

THE NIGHT BEFORE YOUR SESSION

1. Take 2g of magnesium L-threonate the night before your session, at bedtime.

2. Take 4g of vitamin-C the night before your session, at bedtime.

THE DAY OF YOUR SESSION

1. Take 2g of vitamin-C and 2g of magnesium L-threonate the morning before your session. (NOTE: we will provide this at the clinic.)

2. Eating and drinking the day of the session:

☐ Avoid caffeine the day of the session. (Avoid any stimulants.)
☐ Fasting is preferable. If you cannot fast, eat a very light meal one to two hours before your session (e.g., smoothie, banana, etc.).

3. Items to bring:

☐ Wear comfortable clothes (loose fitting), the type you might workout in.
☐ Avoid wearing constricting belts or jeans.

☐ Bring a change of clothes (just in case).

☐ Bring your phone to record your session, if you choose. Make sure you have a voice recording app you are comfortable with. Also, we will make sure you put your phone on airplane mode when recording, because calls and texts can sometimes interfere with voice recording apps.

4. Mental preparation for your session:

It is best to come to this work open and with no expectations. Trust the medicine and your inner wisdom. Also, commit your instructions for MDMA to memory: Trust, surrender, receive.

☐ Trust the medicine
☐ Surrender to the process
☐ Receive what comes up

Trust, surrender, receive. Say that to yourself enough that you can remember it and act on it later.

DURING YOUR SESSION

1. Take Dose 1.

You will get your first dose, which typically (but not always) varies between 100 and 150mg.

2. Relax and surrender to the experience and the medicine.

The medicine takes anywhere from thirty to sixty minutes to become active. It can be difficult to wait for it, but the more you relax, the easier it will be.

3. Take Dose 2 (if needed).

The second dose is typically between 50 to 75mg, and it is usually offered anywhere from sixty to ninety minutes after the first dose. This is optional, though many people take it.

4. Remember the guidelines: Trust, surrender, receive.

There is no agenda. There are no goals. No need for striving. You can completely relax. You can truly surrender. Open your heart. Be open. Be trusting. Be totally open to whatever may arise. It is essential that you trust your inner healing intelligence, which is every person's innate capacity to heal the wounds of trauma.

5. Keep your eye mask on.

You will wear this during the session to help you remain focused inward. The more you can stay focused inward, usually the better the session will be for you.

6. Talk if you feel the need to.

If you feel the need to talk, that is okay as well. Either speak out loud to yourself (being recorded by your phone for you to review later) or speak to your guides. Many people process emotions through talking about them, and if that comes up, that's fine.

7. To use the bathroom:

Sit on the edge of the couch or bed for a minute before you stand up. Even if you feel fine, you may not have good balance at first. Your guide will help you to ensure your safety.

8. Stay with emotions as long as needed.

If something comes up, there's nothing to do but stay with it. Stay with what comes up, stay focused on it, and let it have its say. If necessary, go towards the emotion, engage with it in some way, and allow yourself to examine it and look at it.

One can be literally gifted by the revelations received. And moving through emotional material may not automatically happen just by itself. It may need to be encouraged. You may need to rage, cry, or scream. All of that is fine and will be supported. Ask your guides for any help you feel you need.

1. Eat what you can.

After an MDMA session, people are often not hungry. Try to drink some hydrating juices and any other form of highly absorbable nutrition, such as soup, smoothies, etc. We will help you assess if you are hungry and what to eat.

2. Avoid screens and phones.

Do *not* get on your phone or computer. As much as possible, sit with your emotions and feelings.

3. Practice rest and self-care.

Do nothing but rest and take care of yourself after your session. One of the best ways to perform self-care is to take a bath in epsom salts/magnesium flakes the night after a session (helps to mineralize, clear, relax the body).

4. Use necessary supplements.

If sleep is difficult, then use your melatonin. If you are tense, use more magnesium. If you have a headache, Advil is fine.

THE WEEK AFTER YOUR SESSION

Post-journey supplement regimen:

(This is the usual regimen, pursuant to any contraindications that will be determined by staff.)

☐ Take 400mg of Sam-E each day for the first two days after the session
☐ Then 200mg of Sam-E for Days 3 and 4 after the session
☐ Melatonin and magnesium L-threonate as needed for sleep
☐ 2g of vitamin-C supplementation each day for two days after your session

Post session:

☐ **Rest.** Do not schedule any strenuous social-, work-, or travel-related activities for at least two to three days.
☐ **Avoid stimuli.** Minimize exposure to electronics, large groups/crowds or events, traffic, or triggering situations.
☐ **Slow and steady integration is the key.** A lot will come up. Give it at least a week before you make any major decisions or even solidify the thinking.
☐ **Be good to yourself for a few days, if not forever.** We need to be gentle with ourselves; we are always pushing ourselves.

Recommended integration activities:

☐ Massages, especially from an energetically sensitive or therapeutic body worker, if possible, tend to work great
☐ Acupuncture is also highly recommended; the longer the session, the better
☐ Either talk to your therapist or journal about what came up and how you're going to integrate these lessons into your life
☐ The week after an MDMA session, you are very open, so certain things like energy work or EMDR tend to work very well
☐ Meditation, yoga, floatation, and other activities that, on a regular basis, will provide time for the quality of attention that is conducive to ongoing healing and self-awareness
☐ Record notes or review audio from the session to keep openings salient and active; review intentions in retrospect, in light of what emerged in session
☐ Consider capturing your emotions through journal, art, or movement
☐ Spa and sauna also work well with adequate electrolyte intake and hydration

It takes time.

Understand that the experience catalyzed by the MDMA will likely continue to unfold and resolve over days or even weeks following the session. This unfolding often happens in waves of memories, insights, and/or emotions, some of which may be very affirming and pleasant, and some may be difficult and challenging. It is important that you be prepared for this unfolding and make time in your daily life to attend to this process. Be prepared that other people may not understand the depths of their experience and insights, and for that reason, it is advisable to be discriminating about with whom you share this sensitive material. You may wish to join a support group that is focused on this work.

Journal.

It may be very helpful to write about your MDMA experience and your thoughts and feelings since the session. It's best to write this for yourself without the thought of doing it for anyone else. It also will be helpful to write down your dreams. For some people, MDMA makes dreams more vivid and meaningful.

This is not a "no pain, no gain" situation.

Sometimes moving through waves of painful feelings and memories is part of the unfolding process, but connecting with easy, affirming, pleasurable experiences is part of the healing too and is at least as important as willingness to be with the painful ones.

CHAPTER 10

Alex Begins

It's the day of my session.

I had to use melatonin and magnesium to sleep last night, I was so anxious. I woke up at 5:00 a.m., and I couldn't get back to sleep.

I got up and was about to make coffee, when I remembered: no caffeine.

I drank orange juice, got dressed, and sat on my sofa for an hour watching *SpongeBob Squarepants* to try to get my mind off how anxious I was. I tried the breathing technique, and it helped a little but not as much as it had in Dr. Dan's office.

I re-read the MDMA Therapy Preparation Doc for the twentieth time. I don't think I studied this hard for any test in college.

The taxi pulled up to the clinic at 8:15 a.m. Now I understood why they were so intent on walking me through every step of what I would do the first morning—as soon as I got into the parking lot, my mind went blank.

I forgot everything. Like, I could not remember why I was even there. My mind went blank, the same way it did talking to Dr. Dan that first time and talking to Dr. Kate about whether I wanted to change.

I shook it off, and everything came flooding back.

The receptionist greeted me warmly, and I went back to the sitting room. It was the same familiar combination of a really nice day spa and new age retreat: calm, soothing music, low lights, candles, a relaxing smell, and just a really pleasant vibe. I could feel myself relaxing already.

Dr. Dan came in to greet me, along with Dr. Naomi.

Dr. Dan: "Alex, so glad to see you. How are you feeling?"

Alex: "Kind of nervous to be honest."

Dr. Dan: "That's okay. It's a very common feeling. Allow yourself to feel whatever you're feeling."

He handed me a small dish with a pill in it.

Dr. Dan: "Here is the first thing to take. As we discussed, this is GABA, which we use to help you relax your nervous system. Drink it with water. In it, we've mixed other co-factors, mainly vitamin-C and magnesium."

I took the pills and drank the water mixture.

Dr. Dan: "Feel free to sit here on the sofa and relax. You can read or just practice your breathing exercises. It'll take about thirty minutes for the GABA to start working. Dr. Naomi will stay here to keep you company and talk, and when I come back, we'll start the session. Sound good?"

Alex: "Yep."

I started to freak out a little.

This is almost real now. Is it too late to back out? Can I quit?

I can't quit.

I want to do this, I need to do this, and I told my Pa I would do it.

But seriously, why am I doing this again?

Am I really sweating right now? It's winter time.

Dr. Naomi walked out of the room for a second and then came right back in. She carried two small ceramic dishes, each with a single white pill in them. She set one in front of me and the other behind it and then put a bottle of water next to it.

Dr. Naomi: "How are you feeling?"

Alex: "Great. Perfect. Never been better."

I laughed nervously, and she laughed with me.

Dr. Naomi: "It's very common to feel anxiety at this stage. These two pills I put in front of you are the MDMA. I'm going to go over the basic instructions again, just to make sure you're clear, and answer any last-minute questions."

She ran through everything Dr. Dan had told me, which was the same stuff on the MDMA prep document. I knew everything before she said it, which kind of made me smile. I guessed all my studying for the "test" paid off.

Dr. Naomi: "Do you have any questions?"

Alex: "So…what's the worst thing you've ever seen on MDMA?"

Dr. Naomi: "What do you mean by 'worst'?"

Alex: "I don't know. Like someone dying maybe?"

Dr. Naomi: "Oh no, definitely not. There have been some very intense sessions, but those are often the best sessions. When deep trauma comes up, the process itself may be painful, but the result is always for the better."

Alex: "You did this therapy?"

Dr. Naomi: "Of course. Many times. Every facilitator has done their own work, often for years, before sitting for others. It's absolutely necessary."

Alex: "Why?"

Dr. Naomi: "You can't effectively hold space for another unless you understand what the journey is like. The more work you've done, the better you can help others on their own journey. It's difficult to help others with things you've not addressed in yourself."

Alex: "How many people have you sat for?"

Dr. Naomi: "Not as many as Dr. Dan, but I've sat for a few hundred people."

Alex: "And no real problems?"

Dr. Naomi: "It depends what you mean by 'problems,' but no, nothing unsafe or life-threatening. I think you'll understand more once you take the medicine. The best advice I can give you is to follow the directions: trust, surrender, receive.

"I first did it back when it was illegal, in New York City with an older man named William. He'd been guiding people for decades—all underground, of course.

"He was an amazing guide, so calm and reassuring, and he held such a safe space for me. My session—though challenging in many ways—was the most profound experience of my life. It's why I do this now: to share this healing with others. I think it's the most important work I can do."

I really liked Dr. Naomi. She reminded me of my friend Anne, so calm and confident, radiating serenity. I hadn't even noticed Dr. Dan walk in; I was listening to her so intently.

Dr. Dan: "How are you feeling, Alex?"

Alex: "Better."

Dr. Dan: "Good. If you look under the table, there are several eyeshades. When you feel ready, you can pick one. And if you brought your phone, give it to Dr. Naomi; she'll set it on airplane mode and start recording."

I picked out an eyeshade as Dr. Naomi set up my phone on a side table. Dr. Dan looked at his watch.

Dr. Dan: "The GABA should be taking effect now. Let's do the breathing exercise we practiced, and then we can get started."

We did the same breathing exercise as before. I felt a little dizzy but much more relaxed.

Dr. Dan: "I'm going to invite you to take the medicine any time you'd like. The first dose is the one closest to you."

I looked at the little pill. It looked so normal. It could be anything in my cabinet, like an allergy pill or an aspirin.

Alex: "I half expected you to give me the choice to take a red pill or a blue pill, like Morpheus in *The Matrix*."

We all laughed. I laughed a little too loud, feeling self-conscious and hating it.

Dr. Dan: "It's an apt metaphor. This medicine helps you see how deep the rabbit hole goes, in a sense."

I found myself hesitating, but I got proactive, took the pill out of the ceramic cup, threw it in my mouth, and washed it down. Dr. Naomi looked at her watch and wrote down the time.

Dr. Dan: "If you'd like, now would be a good time to put your eyeshade on and lay back. We're going to turn up the music just a little. Take this time to focus on your breathing as we practiced, and let the medicine do its work."

The music was pretty cool, kind of like the music they play in my favorite Indian restaurant but calmer and more soothing.

Most of my anxiety was gone, at least in my body. Thanks to the GABA, I felt like I'd just been in a hot tub.

As I lay on the sofa with my eyeshade on, my mind started wandering. I thought about how much I loved my dog, and I wished I'd brought her. *Maybe I should ask Dr. Dan about bringing her next time.*

Then, I thought about Pa and how open he'd been with me. Even though we'd been so close, he'd never talked with me like that before. I wondered why.

See, this is why I can't meditate. I can't ever seem to get my thoughts to stop doing this, and most of them are anxious, random thoughts that have nothing to do with anything. Maybe I'm doing it wrong.

How can I sit here for thirty minutes with all these anxious thoughts careening around my head?

My thoughts bounced around like this for what seemed like forever, one thought to another, like a pinball ricocheting all over my mind.

Then, almost out of nowhere, I felt the deepest, purest, most true, most profound love I'd ever felt in my life.

It was like nothing I'd ever felt before. I didn't even realize love could feel like this.

The closest way to describe it would be to say I felt totally complete and whole. I felt connected to everything and one with everything.

This is going to sound stupid, but it felt like...I became love itself.

I said out loud, not really to anyone in particular, "This is amazing. Now I get it."

CHAPTER 11

The Session

As the medicine settled in, waves of love came over me. It was hard to process at first.

Everything was positive. I connected with all the love I felt for everyone in my life, and I was almost in tears about it.

Alex: "This is so amazing. Oh my god, I love everyone."

I started thinking about everyone in my life that I cared about, wanting them to experience this. I started rattling off names, thinking about how amazing it would be for all of them.

Alex: "Oh my God, Pa is going to love this. And Granny too! This will turn her world upside down!"

Dr. Dan: "It's great that you're thinking about these people; it speaks to a deep connection you have to them. But try to focus on yourself right now."

This was nothing like the time I'd done Ecstasy in college. I was shocked at how mentally sharp I felt. Yes, this was an altered state, but I felt full of ideas and totally clear headed. I knew my name, I knew where I was, what time it was, and I felt totally in my right mind.

And the emotions—they were so great, and they kept coming. I didn't know I could feel like this. This intensity of emotion, this depth, the love, the appreciation—all of it.

Alex: "Is the MDMA making my emotions super intense?"

Dr. Dan: "In a sense, yes. But for the most part, it's simply revealing what your emotions really are."

Alex: "Can I feel this way all the time?"

Dr. Dan: "Maybe. Perhaps the intensity would be hard to maintain, but the emotional states of love and acceptance and caring—yes, you absolutely can."

I started to cry.

Alex: "I don't know why I'm crying."

Dr. Dan: "You don't have to know. Perhaps just allow yourself to feel what you're feeling."

Hot tears streamed down my face.

Alex: "I don't know why I'm crying so much."

Then, I felt a big rush of emotion coming, like at the beach, when you can feel the water go out, and you know a big wave is coming.

I didn't know what was coming, but it shifted from a warm, welcoming love to something else. Something heavy, something I didn't want.

I shot up on the sofa and ripped my facemask off.

Dr. Dan and Dr. Naomi were sitting right there, both calm, staring right at me.

I took a few deep breaths. The feeling changed totally. That rush of emotion was gone, and even the intensity was way down.

Alex: "Now I know what you mean when you say MDMA is always your friend. The intensity just went from a ten to a four—in just a few seconds."

They nodded and kept staring at me.

Alex: "I really have to pee."

Dr. Dan: "It's been about an hour, which is normal. Let me help you up; you can be a bit unstable."

He held my arm, and I stood up and walked with him and Dr. Naomi to the bathroom. They helped me walk back when I was done.

Dr. Dan: "Would you like the second dose?"

Alex: "Yeah, I think so."

I took the pill, drank it down, and sat there.

Alex: "This is fucking amazing. My god, why is everyone not doing this? I mean, like, this should be the biggest thing ever. But damn, it's intense, isn't it?"

Dr. Dan: "It is. Would you like to put your eye mask back on and lay back down?"

Alex: "Okay. I'll go back in."

I put my eye mask on, laid back, and made myself a promise: *I'm going to fully surrender to this experience, and let it do what it needs to do.*

CHAPTER 12

The Feelings

The next two hours were indescribable.

I'll try to describe them, but please understand, there are no words that truly explain this. It was so emotional, so full of feeling and expressiveness, that any words are only a faint whisper of what the experience actually *felt* like.

I went on a journey back through my life, seeing and reliving so many events, but this time from a totally different perspective. As if someone had been filming my life and was showing it back to me. Except this time, I could feel what was going on and understand why certain things happened, why I felt the way I did. And all of it was from a place of love, acceptance, and non-judgment.

The big thing it seemed to focus on was how I shut down my emotions. I saw scene after scene in my life where I emotionally shutting down, not allowing myself to feel things. Over and over.

I saw relationships with girls where I did that, or opportunities at work, or times people reached out to me, or interactions with friends. I felt like I was being shown a highlight reel of times I'd emotionally closed myself off.

Then, it shifted. I started seeing painful events. A time my mom yelled at me. A time my dad left me somewhere. But these memories felt very different. They felt so intensely painful. I was actually physically uncomfortable as they came up.

I felt the lightest touch on my ankle.

Dr. Dan: "Alex, how are you doing? You seem to be struggling."

I took off my eyeshade and sat up some.

Alex: "Is what I'm seeing real?"

Dr. Dan: "Does it seem real?"

Alex: "Yeah. I mean, I remember these things happening. They definitely happened."

Dr. Dan: "Are you re-experiencing events or emotions associated with the events? Or both?"

Alex: "The events are the same. But I'm seeing them differently. It's like I'm *feeling* the events. Or the emotions associated with the events. Is that possible?"

Dr. Dan: "Yes. These medicines are also called clarigens because they help us see more clearly. There's actually more blood flow and information and energy going into the memory and emotional centers of your brain. If you saw it and felt it and experienced the memory of it, that sounds real to me. But only you can know."

Alex: "Yeah, it happened. I remember these things. But why are the emotions with them so intense?"

Dr. Dan: "Well, often MDMA helps us unlock the emotion associated with a difficult event, especially if we weren't able to feel it the first time."

Alex: "These memories are of events I thought didn't bother me, but maybe they did. But the feelings are hard stuff to deal with. What does that mean?"

Dr. Dan: "What do you think it means?"

I thought about that for a long time.

Alex: "I'm not exactly sure how, but it seems like the story I've told myself about my life isn't entirely true."

This answer almost felt like it came from a different part of me. From deep inside of me, not from where I usually answer from. It's hard to explain, but this felt like the 'real' me answering.

Alex: "It also means I can uncover my true story. That what I'm seeing is the truth. No, no—what I'm *feeling* is the truth. Or closer to the truth, I guess?"

Dr. Dan: "That's well said. One of the greatest gifts of this medicine is it gives us the ability to have a closer experience of our own personal truth."

I sat and thought about that for a long time. I almost felt the blankness come back, but then a weird thing happened. It was like another part of me set that aside, and I felt warm and loved and safe.

Alex: "I want to receive this truth. It's not very fun though, is it—receiving the truth?"

They both laughed a little.

Dr. Dan: "It can be challenging at first, no doubt. But in my experience, receiving and accepting this truth is what leads to great outcomes. Eventually."

Alex: "I guess this is why I did MDMA therapy: to know these truths and feel them."

Dr. Dan: "Good. In my experience, the best way to do that is to put the eyeshade on and relax into it. It may get rough, but the more you surrender and allow yourself to feel what comes up, the more you get out of it."

Alex: "Yeah, I got it."

I started to put the eyeshade on and then had another thought.

Alex: "I just want to tell you both something: thank you so much for this. Now I know why you do this. This is so important. I can't even explain it, but I get it."

They smiled warmly at me, and we connected for a second, and then I put my eyeshade on and went back in.

Almost immediately, those truths started coming. And some of them were painful and really, really hard to feel.

CHAPTER 13

What Alex Saw

I could almost feel the exact moment the medicine started wearing off. It was like a light switch. I didn't go back to normal, but I definitely felt different all at once. I sat up and took my eye mask off.

Alex: "Wow, I just felt it wear off, kind of."

Dr. Naomi: "It's about five hours past your first dose and four hours past your second, so that makes sense. The medicine is most active for about four hours. But it's not done."

Alex: "I took Ecstasy in college. It was *nothing* like this!"

Dr. Dan: "Yeah, that's a pretty common reaction. The set and setting make a huge difference. And street Ecstasy is usually very impure."

Alex: "What do I do now?"

Dr. Dan: "There's still plenty more to experience if you'd like to stay under the mask. Many people take six or even seven hours. But if you feel the desire to talk, we can do that as well."

Alex: "Yeah, I have a lot of questions. That last part under—that was rough. Just to be clear: there's no chance that this is made up or I'm inventing stuff? Or is there?"

Dr. Dan: "In short, no."

Alex: "So, it's not like mushrooms where I see things that aren't there? Or have weird ideas that have no relationship to reality?"

Dr. Dan: "If you mean does MDMA produce the same types of mental effects as psychedelics, the answer is: no, not really. MDMA doesn't put anything in your head. It simply helps you uncover what's already there."

Alex: "That means I have a lot of stuff to deal with. I saw, or felt, how my parents didn't really care much about me, how petty and childish they are, how concerned they are with material stuff and the opinions of their friend. How sad they are, and how broken they are. I felt how lonely I was, and am, and I saw—sorry, I *felt*—how much it hurt me. If this is true, why didn't I see it before? Or feel it?"

Dr. Dan: "First off, it's great that you're making these insights, and I just want to commend you for really doing the work. I know it probably doesn't feel this way, but you're doing amazing.

"As to why you haven't felt it before—this is how the brain is designed. If, as a child, we have experiences that are really intense and we can't make meaning of them, then we try and defend against them. We tend to build up these walls, what are called 'ego defenses.'

"The core wounds—rejection, abandonment, betrayal, humiliation—can feel so intense that living consistently with that degree of intensity would be too overwhelming. So, we defend against it, build up armor to protect ourselves against them, wall them off, and stick them in the corner. Out of sight, out of mind. Intense emotions are often safer there.

"These medicines help us drop our defenses. We are more available to see and to feel. That stuff we were trying to run from or ignore is still there; now we have the support to be able to feel it and work it through."

Alex: "What do I do with these feelings?"

Dr. Dan: "What do you want to do with them?"

Alex: "I'm not sure. Now I understand what you mean about this being disruptive. This changes everything about how I see my life."

Dr. Dan: "It could."

Alex: "I guess I've been telling myself the story that they've been telling me the whole time, that my mother and father were great parents, but the reality is they're not.

"They didn't do any of the things that 'bad' parents do. They didn't beat me or sexually abuse me or anything like that— thank god—but they didn't seem to care about me very much."

Dr. Dan: "Right now, I would suggest you just sit with it and feel it. Sometimes that's the hardest thing to do: to just be with it, not to have to make it different, not to have to make it right, not to have to heal it, not to have to shut it away, not to have to fix it."

Alex: "Just nothing?"

Dr. Dan: "Feeling your emotions is doing something. It might be the best thing you can do to help heal that young part of yourself. That little boy that just wanted to be loved for who he was, wanted to be recognized and celebrated—perhaps, what he needs is for you to just sit with those feelings."

Alex: "Does this mean my childhood was awful and I was abused? That's the thing, that's what I saw—is that what it means?"

Dr. Dan: "It may be too early to determine its full meaning. You may need to give it space and time and to allow the eventual translation and meaning to come. Sometimes, if we try and make meaning too fast, before we feel it, then we're just trying to help ourselves feel more comfortable by labeling it. It can be helpful to just give yourself a little bit of time and space. You don't have to figure it all out right now."

Alex: "Is it normal that I think I might have more questions now than I did before MDMA?"

Dr. Dan: "It's totally normal."

Alex: "What does that mean?"

Dr. Dan: "It tells me that you're on the path of personal discovery. You're asking really clear, coherent, and important questions. These are all relevant reflections. This is normal and healthy."

Alex: "I'm glad you feel like it's healthy for me, but why does it feel so bad?"

Dr. Dan: "Define 'bad.'"

Alex: "The emotions, the realizations—these aren't pleasant things to think about."

Dr. Dan: "Let's explore the idea of labeling this as 'uncomfortable,' rather than 'good' or 'bad.' This actually might be a good process that you're experiencing something uncomfortable because it's been there the whole time, and it's been impacting how you've lived your life."

Alex: "What do you mean?"

Dr. Dan: "As we discussed, feeling these emotions is the core of the work. Sometimes, the process of getting in touch with uncomfortable experiences can actually be good. It helps us grow and mature and become whole again. Perhaps, these emotions aren't bad. Though painful, perhaps, this is what you need to feel."

Alex: "So, what do I do now?"

Dr. Dan: "Remember the workout analogy we discussed? Muscles need to stretch and tear in order to grow. The act of exercise can be uncomfortable, but it's the only way to improve physical fitness. In this case, you just keep feeling. Simply put: *the only way out is through.*"

Oh damn. Now, *that* I get. That's the only way I've succeeded at anything, really—by working through the hard parts.

Alex: "Okay, I see. I need to feel this because that's how I process it and let it go. You've told me that many times. My therapist too."

I sat and thought about that for a while. It was so simple but really profound. Not labeling these emotions as "bad" but, instead, realizing they're here to teach me a lesson and then trying to learn from them—that's deep.

Alex: "Can I talk about this experience? I still feel the need to discuss it, kind of."

Dr. Dan: "Have you noticed that I almost never tell you what to do? That I almost always just give you suggestions?"

Alex: "Yeah, I did notice that. It weirded me out at first, but now I kinda like it. I didn't realize how many people in my life tell me what I have to do until I met you because it's such a contrast."

Dr. Dan: "Exactly. There are very few times where I'm going to be directive and tell you what to do—and this is one of those:

"I would strongly advise that you not talk about this to anybody—aside from your therapist—for at least a week."

Alex: "Why?"

Dr. Dan: "In short, you've basically just had your entire worldview upended. You've realized that the story you've been telling yourself isn't quite complete. Talking about this with other people will not provide you the space you need to really explore your truth, unpack it, and see what is there.

"When humans talk, most of the conversation is about negotiating a common reality. The more you can sit with this experience yourself, the better you can see your truth first, before you begin to negotiate it with others."

Alex: "But I can talk about it with my therapist?"

Dr. Dan: "For sure. Your therapist is somebody that you have a consistent connection with. Her role is to support you and help you put words to emotional experience.

"By the way, I talked to Dr. Kate a few days ago as we discussed I would. She seems like an excellent therapist."

Alex: "She's pretty great."

I sat and thought for a second, but this nagging question kept coming back.

Alex: "You're saying I shouldn't tell my family about what came up for me?"

Dr. Dan: "I don't think it's the best idea to tell your family, at least during this next week. Let it settle in. Talk to your therapist about it. Get more in touch with this over the next few days while you continue to land the experience, so to speak. Usually after a week or so of integration time, you'll be clearer about what you want to share with your family, if you anything at all."

Alex: "Are the rest of the sessions going to be like this?"

Dr. Dan: "Hard to predict. No two sessions are exactly the same. Each session is a micro-journey along that path."

Alex: "You're saying it's going to get harder?"

Dr. Dan: "No. I'm saying it's going to become more of what it needs to be."

Alex: "That's deep."

Dr. Dan: "Your journey could include more love, more understanding, more compassion, more consideration to a felt experience of what your parents were going through—or a fuller experience of what that younger part of you was going through so that the emotions feel more real and also mobilized in order to be healed and integrated.

"It could be a fuller experience of you now knowing how to more readily connect with the legitimate feelings underneath, like love, throughout all aspects of your life. And it could be a fuller experience of the discomfort and the pain. Yes, that is possible.

"I told you this before: *sometimes it will get harder before it gets easier.*"

Alex: "This whole thing seems crazy."

Dr. Dan: "You've started to peel back the veneer on reality and are now seeing and feeling life in a whole new way."

Yesterday, I would have dismissed that as woo-woo nonsense, but then, I understood.

CHAPTER 14

Recovery

The next week was unlike anything I'd ever experienced.

I did the session on a Friday. Saturday, I laid on my sofa and watched Netflix, and every time an emotion came up, I paused Netflix and journaled about it.

And certain things kept coming back up: memories, insights, emotions, all of it. It was almost like I was still on the medicine but not as intense.

I did this again on Sunday. By the time Monday rolled around, I didn't feel like being around people or going to work, so I took Monday and Tuesday off and kept journaling. Almost every hour, I'd write something down.

By Wednesday, I was feeling normal again but still raw and uncertain. I went to work but made a conscious effort to not talk to anyone. I did see Anne. She was the only one at work that I'd told I was doing MDMA therapy.

Anne: "Wow, you look different."

Alex: "You can tell just from how I look?"

Anne: "Oh yeah. It's hard to describe. You look more…awake? Tired and raw, but your eyes have a different sparkle to them."

Alex: "I feel raw. I've been questioning everything I thought was true and realizing most of it wasn't what I thought. It's so draining."

Anne: "That's normal; it'll pass. Just keep doing your integration work. When you feel ready, I'd love to hear anything you want to share. But not now. Keep it to yourself for now. That's really important."

Alex: "Yeah, Dr. Dan was emphatic about that. I don't even know how to talk about this yet."

Anne: "Don't. It took me weeks before I felt ready to talk about it with anyone."

CHAPTER 15

Therapy Session: "What do you mean I'm traumatized?"

I had a double session booked with Dr. Kate later that day. I was excited but apprehensive. She'd be the first person I talked to about the experience in depth, and so much of what had happened was still raw and fresh in my mind.

Alex: "Soooooo...lots to talk about."

Dr. Kate: "How about we begin with you telling me everything you want to about your session. I will listen, and then we'll discuss it, okay?"

I told her every detail I could remember and what I'd done since. I trusted her, so I held nothing back. I talked for at least twenty minutes straight. That was why she wanted a double session, I guess.

Dr. Kate: "Sounds like you had a very intense and moving session."

Alex: "I don't even know where to start evaluating it."

Dr. Kate: "We can start by just recognizing where you are and what you did. You made a serious commitment to yourself to change, and you followed through. That's fantastic.

"Second, it sounds like you surrendered to the process and let feelings come up that were painful,but necessary. That's very difficult to do as well, and I commend you."

Wow. I *had* made a commitment to myself and done the hard work to keep it. I hadn't thought about it like that, but it was true.

Alex: "But wow, it was still rough."

Dr. Kate: "The first session often is. How do you feel?"

Alex: "I don't know where to start. I feel confused. I feel angry. I feel sad. I feel overwhelmed. You did this therapy, right? You know what it's like."

Dr. Kate: "I do, but this isn't my session. The worst thing I could do is tell you what I felt or talk about my experience. The best thing I can do is make space for you and help you understand your own experience."

I totally got her point, but damn, I really wanted her to kind of tell me what she went through—I guess because I was having so much trouble understanding my experience.

Alex: "I don't know what to think."

Dr. Kate: "Okay."

Alex: "No, that's not it. I feel like a bomb just went off in my emotions, and I don't know how to deal with the chaos. I mean, I feel like in some ways, my whole reality just collapsed."

Dr. Kate: "In some ways, it did."

Alex: "I realized the stories I've told myself aren't true. Can that really be? Have I been fooling myself this whole time about everything?"

Dr. Kate: "You wouldn't be the first. This is a very common experience."

Alex: "This sounds weird to say, but...I felt so full of love at one point. Is it possible that might have been the first time I ever felt real love in my life?"

Dr. Kate: "Absolutely, it's possible."

Alex: "Does it mean no one's loved me? I thought I'd felt love, you know, from my parents and definitely from my grandparents, but did I not?"

Dr. Kate: "What do you think it means?"

Alex: "My parents always told me they loved me...I didn't actually *feel* any love. And on the medicine, it was like...I felt that lack of love. Is that possible?"

Dr. Kate: "Based on everything I know about you, that sounds accurate."

Alex: "Does this mean they were bad parents? What does this mean about me?"

Dr. Kate: "Let's hold off on what it means. That's important, and we'll get to it later. For now, tell me more about your experience."

Alex: "The love was contrasted with this intense loneliness. And sadness. Like I was just empty inside. I felt all this pain come up. It was crazy, though, Dr. Kate; I don't think of myself as a depressed person. Where did all this pain and sadness even come from?"

Dr. Kate: "Isn't that why you did MDMA therapy? Because you felt empty and sad all the time, and nothing was helping you?"

Alex: "When you put it that way…yeah…but that sounds so bad."

Dr. Kate: "What bothers you about the way it sounds?"

Alex: "I don't know. I don't want to think of myself as depressed, I guess."

Dr. Kate: "What if you are?"

It felt like she punched me in the gut. Not the way she said it—that was kind. But like, the words themselves. They hit me. I think she saw it on my face because she didn't even wait for me to respond.

Dr. Kate: "Most people misunderstand depression. Many people think of it as being sad all the time."

Alex: "Isn't it?"

Dr. Kate: "That's a good enough understanding of what depression feels like in the moment. But the real question is why someone is depressed."

Alex: "It's got to depend on the person, right?"

Dr. Kate: "The specifics do, yes. But overall, depression works the same in almost all people:

"Depression comes from a denial of one's own emotions."

Time completely stopped. Her sentence kept echoing back in my head:

Depression comes from a denial of one's own emotions.

It was like this unlocked a new level in my head or something. All at once, I realized that I *had* been depressed most of my life and hadn't wanted to see it. That's exactly what I saw and felt in my session: my real emotions.

My head was spinning. I was alternating between going blank and being flooded with emotions. Then, I realized—I had water leaking out of my eyes.

Alex: "Am I crying?"

Dr. Kate: "This is a good sign, Alex. In over a year of therapy, I've never once seen you cry or, really, be emotional at all."

Alex: "HOW IS ME CRYING A GOOD THING?!"

Dr. Kate gave me a look I've never seen from her: deep, motherly compassion.

I knew that look. I've seen it before. From Granny Jane.

That made me cry even more.

Dr. Kate handed me some tissues and let me sit there and cry. I don't know how long I cried. I'm not really even sure what I cried about.

Alex: "I feel like I'm falling apart. I feel totally out of control."

Dr. Kate: "This is what it feels like to be sad. As you said, you've denied your own emotions for most of your life, and it appears that the medicine has helped you finally connect with what you actually feel."

Alex: "I don't want this. I feel crazy."

Dr. Kate: "You're not crazy. You're simply feeling your emotions. If anything, this is the opposite of crazy. I deal with crazy every day; I would tell you if you were. You're not."

I laughed because that was the fucking truth—Dr. Kate really would have told me. She didn't pull punches.

That was both what annoyed me about her and made me keep coming back. She was so honest—but honest in the way that you can't get mad or defensive. She was just like a mirror but still kind about it.

I sat there crying, feeling completely discombobulated and laughing about not being crazy. Which made me feel crazier.

Dr. Kate: "Have you considered the possibility that you have a lot of trauma that you've never processed—or even accepted—as part of your life?"

Alex: "Now I do. That came up on the medicine. I felt such deep despair and loneliness. I felt like...*I didn't have parents?* Never mind, I feel stupid saying it."

Dr. Kate: "Let me throw this idea out. I'm not saying it's true or not, I'm simply throwing it out as an idea to play with:

"What if you didn't have parents?

"I don't mean that literally. Obviously, you did have parents. Let's just play with the idea, on a metaphorical level."

Alex: "What do you mean?"

Dr. Kate: "What comes up for you when you think about the absence of parents?"

I felt myself getting defensive.

Alex: "I didn't mean anything. It was stupid. My parents weren't bad people. Other people had it way worse. I hate people who always blame everything on their parents; I'm not like that."

Dr. Kate: "I never said your parents were bad people. They might have been great people. And other people definitely had it worse. And you are absolutely right that blaming others for your problems is an ineffective way to deal with life.

"Remember, we're just playing around with an idea that came up for you in your medicine session—that you didn't have parents. What happens if you let yourself sit with that idea?"

Alex: "Yeah, I felt that, but that's ridiculous. Obviously, I had parents."

Dr. Kate: "Yes, you had parents. But tell me again what you felt when this thought came up."

Alex: "I don't know. I felt all this deep sadness and loneliness. Grief maybe? Does that make sense? What am I grieving, though?"

Dr Kate: "If you had to guess, what would you guess that you're grieving?"

Alex: "My lonely childhood?"

Dr. Kate: "That makes a lot of sense."

Alex: "Yeah, maybe they weren't the best parents in a lot of ways that I didn't understand before, but it wasn't that bad, was it? I'm feeling all this sadness, but come on, this isn't like I have PTSD. This isn't real trauma."

Dr. Kate: "How do you know that?"

Alex: "What?"

Dr. Kate: "How do you know you don't have what you call 'real trauma'?"

Alex: "What do you mean? I have a regular life. I never went to war. I wasn't raped or beaten or anything like that. My parents never hit me or starved me or put me in a cage or anything. I don't have any real trauma. Come on, be serious!"

Dr. Kate: "Do you think that's the only way to suffer trauma?"

Alex: "Isn't it?"

Dr. Kate: "Not at all. Would you like me to explain what trauma is and how it works?"

Alex: "Yeah, of course. I thought it was, like, physical and sexual abuse."

Dr. Kate: "That's a common misconception, and it often impedes people from growth. Let me explain:

"Trauma is a nearly universal part of the human experience. Everyone suffers from it, at least to some degree.

"Most people usually think of trauma as a thing that happens in very extreme circumstances—rape, molestation, physical abuse, war, physical violence, domestic violence, or natural disasters. Those are all definitely trauma, but they are a specific kind of trauma and not the only kind."

Alex: "Right, I've never had any of that happen to me."

Dr. Kate: "There are other forms of trauma, and they can be just as bad, if not worse. There are physical traumas, emotional traumas, social traumas, and attachment traumas. A major source of trauma for many people is chronic emotional neglect.

"For example, there's a lot of research that's shown that such neglect can be just as damaging to children as physical abuse and sexual molestation. I can think of one famous study that followed children from birth to twenty years old. The researchers thought that classically abusive behavior like yelling and hitting by mothers would be the strongest indicator of mental instability in their adult children.

"Instead, they found that a mother's emotional withdrawal had the most profound and long-lasting impact. Neglect. Not physical or even sexual abuse.

"Another example, there was a landmark study called Adverse Childhood Experiences study, which found that only one third of people had *not* suffered some sort of serious trauma as a child.

"The trauma numbers for our society go far beyond what most people realize. Childhood trauma—from all sources—is a serious epidemic.

"Some people have argued that it is *the* epidemic, the root cause of so many other issues. I think that argument has a lot of merit."

Alex: "Wait, neglect is traumatic?"

Dr. Kate: "Neglect in children is always traumatic to some degree and can be horrific for children, yes. You don't have to rely on my word; you're welcome to read the primary sources. I'm happy to give you a list of books about this if you'd like."

Alex: "Yeah, that'd be cool."

I paused and thought about this.

Alex: "But what does all this mean for me?"

Dr. Kate: "I can't tell you that. What I'm trying to do now is simply help you understand information that will assist you as you determine what it means to you, if anything."

Alex: "Can you tell me more about childhood trauma from neglect? Not mine specifically—I just mean in general. This is a new idea for me."

Dr. Kate: "Of course. It's new for a lot of people. Let's take a step back and define trauma, so you know what I mean.

"Trauma is an injury caused by fright, helplessness, loss, overwhelming fear, or possibly even lack of control. Trauma happens when this fear injury causes an autonomic nervous system response that stays unresolved.

"It's not a disease or a disorder, just an injury. This is why many psychologists argue that PTSD should actually be called PTSI—post-traumatic stress injury.

"The best book that explains this is called *The Body Keeps the Score* by Bessel van der Kolk. He explains exactly how this process works.

"The book that really opened my eyes was Peter Levine's book *In an Unspoken Voice: How the Body Releases Trauma and Restores Goodness*. The classic example that Peter Levine gives is from nature. You watch nature shows, right?"

Alex: "Are you kidding? My dog and I watch those like we're getting paid to."

Dr. Kate: "You know in the show when a lion chases a gazelle? It's intense for a second, but the gazelle gets away? You see what it does after it's away right? It shakes itself off."

Dr. Kate did this motion where she went into a quick, spazzy, full-body movement, and I started laughing. It was hilarious, and she was laughing with me. But it reminded me of something.

Alex: "Yes! That's *exactly* what Murph, my dog, does when she meets a dog she doesn't like at the dog park. As she walks away, she shakes it off. That's her 'fight' energy from 'fight, flight, or freeze.' Then, she seems fine."

Dr. Kate: "Exactly right. That's 'fight' energy. All three responses are deeply ingrained biological responses to survival threats— fight, flight, and freeze. When we are able to get the response out, then we are fine. But when we don't, it gets stuck in the body and causes all kinds of problems."

Alex: "I think I get it."

Dr. Kate: "Let me explain with another example you will reso- nate with personally:

"If you and your girlfriend have a long talk and decide to break up, that will be sad for you. But it won't be traumatic. You'll get over it.

"But imagine if your girlfriend sends you a text out of nowhere saying, "You're dumped" and then refuses to talk to you or engage you again. That could create an unresolved autonomic response and, thus, be potentially traumatic. Can you see the difference?"

Alex: "Oh yes, most definitely. That exact scenario happened to me in college. And it's right. The breakups, where we talked—it was no big deal. The one where I didn't, that was really hard to deal with. I did nothing for weeks and was sad and depressed."

Dr. Kate: "That's energy that gets 'stuck,' so to speak. When an animal gets a deep fear and can't run or fight, all that's left is to freeze."

Alex: "What's funny is that after that happened, I froze my ass to the sofa and watched TV and ate Cheetos for a month. It was terrible."

Dr. Kate: "One thing to understand is that trauma is about the nervous system's response to an event, not necessarily the event itself. Events can affect each of us very differently.

"That's why some soldiers can come back from war fine but others never get past it. It's not the event that's necessarily traumatic; it's the way both the body and the mind handle it and whether the body is able to let the trauma go.

"But regardless, all of us have traumas in our lives. Every single one."

Alex: "I don't get it. Then, why are some people okay and others aren't?"

Dr. Kate: "Let me say first that this isn't a resolved issue in science. A lot of people have a lot of different opinions about this. I can only tell you what I believe after decades of studying this and treating many, many trauma survivors in clinical practice, as well as dealing with my own traumas.

"I believe it's because of how they handle the traumas. People who feel the emotions from the trauma and work through them are able to release it.

"But for those that do not work through it, the trauma can—in essence—get stuck in their body.

"Alcoholics Anonymous has a saying: 'The issues are in the tissues,' and that's quite literally scientifically true. The energy of the trauma seems to get physically stuck in the body."

Alex: "So, what does this have to do with me and my issues?"

Dr. Kate: "Everything. Our childhood traumas are not really formed by the actual events that happen to us. These traumas form by the feelings left unprocessed in the absence of an empathic witness. Trauma teaches you to survive these intense emotions by coping, defending, and avoiding being triggered. Healing teaches you to thrive by feeling, releasing, and owning your triggers."

Alex: "Explain that more please. I don't get it."

Dr. Kate: "Brain-imaging studies of trauma patients find unusual activity in an area of the brain called the insula, which regulates basic survival needs by integrating and interpreting information from the body's sensory organs and transmits 'fight, flight or freeze' signals to the amygdala when necessary.

"In people with stored trauma, these signals are firing *all the time*. There is no conscious influence; people who have unresolved trauma constantly feel on edge for no apparent reason.

"They may have a sense that something has gone wrong or a feeling of imminent doom. Does that sound familiar?"

Alex: "Are you kidding? Of course."

Dr. Kate: "The overall effect of trauma is usually described as a loss in the feeling of aliveness, motivation, excitement, and purpose.

"This is because trauma robs people of agency. Self-leadership. The feeling that you're in charge of yourself.

"People who have parents that ignored their needs learn to anticipate rejection and withdrawal. They cope by blocking out their anger or rage or fear or shame and by acting as if it doesn't matter.

"But 'the body keeps the score': it remains in a state of high alert, prepared to ward off blows, deprivation, or the experience of core wounds like abandonment, rejection, and betrayal.

"And this is shown in brain scans. Those with chronic PTSI have almost no activation of what are called the 'self-sensing' areas of the brain when compared to non-traumatized subjects. They are dark.

"What this means is that people who suffer intense traumas and are not able to release the energy from them, shut down the feeling sections of their brains. The emotions and feelings of the unresolved trauma are overwhelming, and so they, in effect, 'turn them off' so they can survive.

"Which makes sense—if you are constantly feeling the pain of the trauma, your body and mind can't handle it. It has to turn it off to go on."

Alex: "This is what people mean by emotional dissociation, right?"

Dr. Kate: "Yes, this is an intense version of it. That's a rough trade off though: in order to shut off the terror of trauma, the PTSI victims also shut off all emotions and, thus, their ability to feel anything good.

"To get rid of the bad feelings, they lose contact with all *other feelings.*

"This is why so many trauma victims report feeling so empty inside."

That's me. She's describing me.

My god…have I really turned off all my emotions to avoid the hard ones?

Dr. Kate: "Also, traumatized people often do not have a clear sense of purpose and direction because they can't check in with themselves about what they truly want. Since they can't feel anything in their bodies, they don't know what they want.

"Emotions like desire and passion and contentment drive us to our purpose, and without being able to feel these emotions, we can't know what we enjoy or don't enjoy—in effect, we don't know who we are."

Alex: "This is me. This is exactly me."

Dr. Kate: "This is especially true for children. Children need confidence—confidence that others will know, affirm, and cherish them.

"Without that, they can't develop a sense of agency that will enable them to assert what they believe in, what they stand for, or what they will devote themselves to.

"If a child feels safely held in the hearts and minds of the people who love them, they will feel they can do anything—and probably can, within the range of their skills."

I felt weak.

I wasn't sure why until I realized it was an emotion—and one I don't think I've felt for a long time:

Relief.

Alex: "I'm relieved right now. Why?"

Dr. Kate: "Press into it. You tell me why you're relieved."

Alex: "Because now I know why I constantly feel like I'm dead inside. Now I know I have emotions, but they're hidden from trauma. Now I get it."

Dr. Kate: "Exactly. I've been hoping for a long time that you'd be able to understand this."

Alex: "What? Why didn't you just tell me this?"

She gave me that knowing look again, the one she always gives me.

Dr. Kate: "If I'd have told you this two months ago, how would you have taken it?"

I immediately laughed.

Alex: "Okay, I get it. I wasn't ready to see it. Actually, I wasn't ready to *feel* it."

I sat with this for a while and tried to process the firehose of realizations that I felt coming at me.

Alex: "This is mind blowing. I still don't think I get it really, but I am starting to see it."

Dr. Kate: "This is how therapy works. The more of it you realize yourself, the better it is. All I can really do is help you have your own realizations, as you're ready to make them.

That, and I can care about you and connect with you as a person, to help you explore your feelings in a safe and accepting place. That's all we really do as therapists. That's what the term 'holding space' actually means."

I'd never thought about it like that.

Dr. Kate: "It's kind of a strange paradox. This is called 'talk therapy,' but the actual talking is very little of the work. Most of the work is between the words."

Alex: "What do you mean? That's all we do is talk."

Dr. Kate: "Hardly, though I can understand why you think that."

Alex: "What do you mean?"

Dr. Kate: "Remember how you talked about feeling blank? That's what trauma does. It shuts you down."

Alex: "Oh damn…of course. So, you're saying I am noticing my trauma?"

Dr. Kate: "You are noticing the effect of it, how it shuts you down. Trauma is not easy to see. If your brain is hiding the trauma feelings from you so that you can function, how can you even know they are there? Only indirectly. Blankness is one trauma response.

"Other trauma responses can be ADD-type behaviors, extreme emotional reactions, addictive behaviors, and almost anything done to regulate your nervous system and calm it down."

Alex: "But why does it work like this?"

Dr. Kate: "No one is precisely sure. There is so much we don't know about trauma. My best guess, based on research and clinical experience, is that because trauma overwhelms the body, unless you're able to deal with it in the moment, your body 'hides' it, in a sense, to keep you safe and alive.

"We do know that trauma exists in the mind in a very different place from language, and there has never been an effective treatment for trauma that only involved talking about it."

Alex: "Really? Why not?"

Dr. Kate: "Alex, you can't talk your way out of something you did not talk your way into."

Alex: "That makes total sense."

Dr. Kate: "Most people with PTSI can tell a coherent story about their trauma and even experience the pain associated with the trauma.

"But they often continue to be haunted by unbearable images and physical sensations. No matter how much insight or understanding they develop, the rational part of their brain cannot talk the emotional brain out of its felt reality.

"To put it as simply as possible:

"We don't think emotions; we feel emotions. Thus, you can't talk your way out of trauma; you must *feel* your way out of trauma.

"We use talking to try to help you feel those feelings, but the feeling is the work, not the talking. That's why I say the work is between the words."

Alex: "Damn, that is so obviously true, but I'd never even considered it."

Dr. Kate: "Most people haven't. Another simple example: 90 percent of your serotonin receptors are in your gut, not your brain. Thus, the term 'gut feeling.' Because you are literally feeling it in your gut. Roughly speaking: thinking is in your brain. Feeling is in your body."

Alex: "Yeah, I learned about serotonin receptors in the gut in biopsych in college. Why did they not explain it like this?"

Dr. Kate: "Because most people don't really know it."

Alex: "So, what does this mean?"

Dr. Kate: "It means that if you want to get past your trauma, you must feel your emotions surrounding it so that you can let them go and then integrate the experience into yourself.

"That's why Dr. Dan told you that MDMA might make things worse before they get better.

"This medicine does not erase bad memories or even neutralize them. It opens you up and brings the bad memory and corresponding difficult emotion to the surface, so you can actually feel it and let your body have the healing response it could not have when the event happened. The medicine helps you match the emotion to the experience."

Oh my god. That is exactly *what I felt during my session.*

Alex: "Why didn't he explain it to me like that?"

Dr. Kate: "I don't want to speak for him, but my guess is he wanted you to feel it for yourself so that it would really sink in.

"This is the sort of realization that can't be fully explained, it has to be felt. He knew you would feel it on the MDMA and then be able to realize it that way.

"All I'm doing now is providing you a frame around what you felt, within the context of our safe and trusting relationship, so you can really explore it."

Alex: "What do you mean?"

Dr. Kate: "I already told you that in order to really heal trauma, you must feel the feelings behind it, so you can let them go, right?"

Alex: "Yeah."

Dr. Kate: "Okay, there's a bit more to that.

"Feeling the feelings by itself is often not enough. You must feel the feelings in a safe emotional place, usually with an empathic witness.

"Going back to trauma by itself does not always release it. Usually, you must provide the brain with a new option.

"You create a new experience of that trauma where, instead of getting stuck in it, you have an empathic witness who helps ensure your needs are met and your longings for love are validated.

"You basically tell your emotional brain that it's safe to go back to the trauma and re-experience it because now you have the love and support you need to be able to let it go.

"That's a deep simplification, of course, but that's what therapy is, at its core."

Alex: "This is mind-blowing."

Dr. Kate: "That's the usual reaction when people finally get it."

Alex: "So, if I have suffered trauma, what does this mean about my parents?"

Dr. Kate: "I have no idea. Maybe nothing. Maybe a lot. You'll have to think and feel into that as you integrate your feelings into your new understanding of yourself.

"But, honestly, that isn't what matters because this isn't about them. This isn't their life or their trauma. This is yours only. Regardless of their role in your trauma, even if they were amazing parents or not the best parents—that doesn't really matter to the issue at hand.

"You will get a good understanding of all that if you keep doing this work, but *how* the facts end up coming out doesn't matter to the core reality of your work:

"This is your trauma, and it's your responsibility to work through it."

I sat and thought about it some more and then almost spontaneously said it without thinking about it.

Alex: "Yeah, maybe I have been traumatized."

CHAPTER 16

Resting, Relaxing... and Feeling

I spent the next few days doing nothing but laying on my sofa or walking my dog.

The only other thing I did was listen to my session with Dr. Kate. She records our sessions for me, and thank god she does. Before this, I never listened to them, but this time I probably listened to that session at least ten times. Every time I listened to it, I learned more, and I made more connections.

Some of those lines she said really hit home the more I thought about them:

Depression comes from a denial of one's own emotions.

What if you didn't have parents?

Here's the problem with turning off the negative feelings from trauma: it also turns off all other feelings.

This is your trauma, and it is your responsibility to work through it.

Other than listening to that session again and again, I didn't do much of anything else. I didn't write; I didn't do my breathing; I didn't read any of the books Dr. Kate mentioned. I just listened to our session, thought about what she said, and tried to feel what I was feeling.

I found myself swinging wildly between all sorts of emotional extremes: anger one minute, sadness the next, laughing, then crying. I cried at a damn baby food commercial, and I had no idea why! I felt like a crazy person.

Maybe this is worse than I thought?

And if it is, what does that mean?

About me, about my family, about my relationships to them?

CHAPTER 17

Integration Session 1: "How do I face this?"

I had my first integration session with Dr. Dan on Friday morning, two days after my session with Dr. Kate. This was exactly one week after my MDMA therapy session.

Dr. Dan: "Let's start with how the last week has been for you."

Alex: "It's been an absolute roller coaster, Dr. Dan. I've felt every emotion possible, more intensely than I've ever felt them: anger, rage, sadness, agony, loneliness, despair, abandonment, betrayal, disappointment."

"I feel like a Band-Aid has been ripped off a wound I didn't know I had, but it wasn't a wound. It was my whole life."

Dr. Dan: "That sounds hard."

Alex: "Apparently, I suffered a lot of trauma as a kid."

Dr. Dan: "Is that news to you?"

Alex: "I mean...in a way, yes. I assume you know all about trauma, and how it works, and getting stored in the body, and making you go blank, and all of that research, of course?"

Dr. Dan: "Oh yes. You've been reading about that this week?"

I explained my session with Dr. Kate, everything I had learned.

Dr. Dan: "As I told you, in my discussion with Dr. Kate, I experienced her as an excellent therapist. That all sounds very accurate to me, and I agree completely."

Alex: "I gotta be honest, Dr. Dan: in some ways, this whole thing has me feeling worse than I did before."

Dr. Dan: "That's a pretty common reaction at this stage of the treatment."

Alex: "Half of me wishes I could go back. The other half is glad to know the truth but wishes I wasn't hurting so much. It's funny I made that *Matrix* joke. You know what happens after he takes the red pill, and he wakes up in that awful wasteland of reality, right? I feel like that."

I paused and looked down. Even talking about my emotions was hard.

Alex: "I guess that's where I am. I guess I'm glad that I know the truth, but the truth is pretty awful, and I don't know what to do about it."

Dr. Dan: "This may sound unusual, but I'm excited about your process."

I must have given him a weird look because he laughed at me.

Dr. Dan: "In my experience, this is how the work starts. This is what it feels like when you wake up from the delusion.

"Let's stay with the *Matrix* analogy since you know that movie so well. If we take that analogy of *The Matrix* one step further, Neo took the red pill so as to step into his power and to become who he was here to become.

"When he woke up, he needed complete restoration of his physical body then retraining of his mind. It took time, and it was painful at first."

Alex: "Yeah, but does it have to suck this much?"

Dr. Dan laughed at that.

Dr. Dan: "Sometimes it does. The reason I get excited about this for you—your process and not your pain—is because you're in the midst of uncovering truth. You have a window right now. You're starting to see more of the truth of your life.

"Before, you were maybe in the black where you were in delusion, confusion, disconnection from all of this emotional material. Now, you're moving up into a greater experience of truth.

"You're just seeing one part of the truth—which yeah, it was shitty. There were ways that your needs weren't met. There were ways that you weren't loved.

"If we're here to wake up fully to the totality of who we are, we don't get to select which emotions we're going to feel."

Alex: "Yeah, I get it. But I feel like I've done nothing but suffer this week."

Dr. Dan: "Life includes suffering. That's an unavoidable fact. And if you've been running from your suffering for years, pushing it away and pretending it's not there—guess what? When it catches up to you, it's going to be a lot. You have a 'suffering debt' to pay, so to speak."

Alex: "Man, do I. It feels overwhelming."

Dr. Dan: "I've been there. Life is feeling emotions, and you have not been feeling them for a long time. Now that you are, yes, it can be overwhelming, and yes, it can be hard, but this will pass, and you will come through it. The road to heaven usually goes through hell first."

Alex: "But how? How do I do this?"

Dr. Dan: "There's an old proverb: *how do you eat an elephant?*"

Alex: "Uhhh…I have no idea."

Dr. Dan: "One bite at a time."

Alex: "Oh. Yeah."

Dr. Dan: "The solution to suffering is waking up from the delusion and seeing things more accurately and truthfully and feeling all the emotions that come from that suffering.

"Feel your grief. Feel your pain. Feel your sadness and letdowns. Feel your anger."

Alex: "Okay, but like…this might be a stupid question, but how do I do that?"

Dr. Dan: "What other movies do you like? What other myths or heroes are your favorites, or do you relate to?"

Alex: "I like *Gladiator*. *Maximus* was pretty cool. I like *8-Mile*. Eminem was great in that. I loved *Harry Potter* as a kid, of course."

Dr. Dan: "I'm familiar with those stories. Each of those characters—Maximus, Eminem, and Harry Potter—all had to go on a hard journey and face external enemies. And they also had internal obstacles as well. And for all three of them, the most deep and powerful obstacles were the internal ones. Their own emotions."

I thought about that.

For Maximus, he had to deal with his grief over his betrayal, the death of his family, and how he would face his own death.

For Eminem, he had to confront all the negative things about himself and admit them publicly to win the rap battle.

And for Harry, man, he had nothing but emotional problems: loneliness, abandonment, isolation, fear, grief—all of it. Yeah, there was this old wizard trying to kill him, but like, he didn't really have to face him until the end of the books. Those battles were almost anti-climactic compared to his struggle with his own emotions.

I'd never thought about it like that.

Dr. Dan: "You're on the same journey. The only real difference is that each of those characters had external enemies. In our modern world, we don't really have many of those anymore. There isn't a Commodus or Voldemort or someone like that. Our enemy is, in a sense, inside ourselves."

Alex: "That's some deep shit, Dr. Dan."

Dr. Dan: "The rabbit hole goes very deep. So, to answer your question, how do you get in touch with your emotional landscape? One day at a time, one emotion at a time. You sit with the emotions, you feel them, you give them their say, and then you let them pass."

I sat and thought about that for a long time. It was pretty much what Dr. Kate had told me just the day before.

They were both probably onto something, but still, my mind felt resistant and somewhat blank, which I learned is a sign of my trauma blocking my emotions.

Alex: "Is there anything you can give me to do that might help me work through this when I'm in it? I mean, aside from the breathing. A way to think?"

Dr. Dan: "Are you spiritual? Meaning, do you believe in God?"

Alex: "I guess. I'm not really religious, but I am spiritual."

Dr. Dan: "I ask because this acronym I'm about to give you puts some atheists off, but if you believe in God, it might be really good for you. Every time you're feeling a hard emotion come up, remember the acronym RISEN.

"RISEN:

"**Recognize** the emotion that has risen up in you.

"**Investigate** it with curiosity and no judgment.

"**Slow down** and breathe into it.

"**Express** it in its own way, which is usually feeling it.

"**Neutralize** it by letting it go, once you're ready.

"Then, if it feels right, turn towards a more comfortable feeling (for example, peace, forgiveness, gratitude, love, etc.). See if that works for you."

Alex: "I like specific instructions. RISEN: recognize, investigate, slow down, express, neutralize. I can remember that. I can do that."

Dr. Dan: "And keep your journey in mind.

"You're a hero, at least to yourself. You are going on a journey to discover yourself. You have answered a call to our own adventure, and this call you have answered is a soul-level journey that you must go on in order to be more of who you truly are. But you can't become fully whole without sacrifices, without suffering, without the pain of realization and rebirth.

Harry and Maximus and Eminem had to go through this process, which some people call 'dark night of the soul,' just like you are now. This is part of the process to get in touch with who we are down deep, at the core of our being."

Alex: "Is that what this is, the dark night of my soul?"

Dr. Dan: "Maybe. Or maybe not. I don't think this is the totality of it. This is the beginning, where you realize that this journey will be hard. There is probably more coming. And it may get harder."

Alex: "It's going to get worse?"

Dr. Dan: "It can, but it depends on what you mean by 'worse.' Again, this is not bad. This is the way. We know that our greatest obstacles are our best teachers. They tend to show us more about ourselves, help us grow into our greatness, beyond what we thought was possible. And it's only when suffering is divorced from meaning that it becomes overwhelming and unbearable for people.

"This is why it's important to know what you're going for, what's your 'why,' and keep coming back to your 'why.' Where's the purpose and meaning in it?"

Alex: "At the beginning, my only purpose was to feel better. But that's not very inspiring, is it?"

Dr. Dan: "Ask yourself: 'why do I want to go on this journey?'"

I went blank again.

Alex: "I don't know."

Dr. Dan: "That's okay. You'll find an answer eventually. Once you do, keep anchoring into that, and you'll find the motivation to stay on the journey.

"If you lose it from time to time, that's totally okay too. That's why we're having these conversations. That's why you've orchestrated me to be in your support team and your therapist to be in your support team. All of this is necessary.

"We must go on this journey ourselves, but we can't do it alone."

Alex: "Yeah, I get that. It's up to me, but I can get help. Like Luke Skywalker blew up the Death Star, but he had a ton of help from other people."

Dr. Dan: "Exactly."

Alex: "So, if I'm Luke Skywalker here, would that make you Yoda?"

Dr. Dan laughed with me.

Dr. Dan: "I can be your Yoda here, yes."

Alex: "I want to talk about purpose more. I'm not sure I had a real clear purpose coming in other than I didn't like my life. It's not a very strong purpose, just wanting to feel better, is it?"

Dr. Dan: "Remember when we talked about intention versus expectation? Get clear on the 'what,' get clear on the 'why,' and let go of the 'how' and the 'when.' Does that make sense?"

Alex: "I think so."

Dr. Dan: "Are you clear on your 'why'?"

Alex: "I don't know. I don't think so."

Then, out of nowhere, an image popped into my head. It was fully formed and almost like a movie, but it was there.

I felt embarrassed talking about it, but Dr. Dan was staring at me, so I let it rip.

Alex: "My future family. My future wife and my future kids and our future together."

Dr. Dan: "That's a very powerful purpose."

Alex: "I have no idea where that came from though. I don't even have a girlfriend."

Dr. Dan: "You don't have to know all of that right now. But the coolest part about your story is that you get to write it yourself. You've taken up your pen and started working on a new story already, even if you don't realize it."

Alex: "I feel kind of ridiculous talking about a life that doesn't exist."

Dr. Dan: "Well, the first step in a new life is often envisioning it."

Alex: "Yeah, that's true. But what if I'm confused about what I want?"

Dr. Dan: "I think confusion is what happens at an inflection point. We realize we can't live the way we've been living. It's no longer okay. That's what drove you here.

"When we start to sprout and come out of that little bud, it's going to feel vulnerable. It's going to feel confusing. It's going to feel like maybe we made the wrong choice because the usual safeguards aren't in place anymore. But if you keep going, you'll find it all works out.

"Milton Erickson said once that enlightenment is always preceded by confusion."

Alex: "So, all I can really do right now is keep doing what I'm doing. Stay with the emotions, deal with them and keep working through the process?"

Dr. Dan: "Yep. It takes a lot of courage to do this work. It takes a lot of faith to do this work. It takes a lot of strength to do this work. Where you're at right now is exactly where you most need to be."

Alex: "If you say so."

I still felt so confused, so many conflicting emotions washing over me.

Alex: "It seems to me like sitting with emotions isn't doing anything except make me feel crazy. But I'll try."

Dr. Dan: "With emotions, just feeling them is very much doing something."

Alex: "Dr. Dan, can I ask you an honest question?"

Dr. Dan: "Please do."

Alex: "What if I want to quit now? Like, would you think bad of me?"

Dr. Dan: "No, never. I'm proud of you for coming this far, and I would never look down on anyone for any decision they made about this work when they feel it's best for them. My role here is to support you in whatever you decide.

"And even if you did stop, once you've seen what's down the rabbit hole, you can't unsee it. You've still made massive progress, regardless of what happens in the future with medicine work. Especially if you keep your integration practice up, there's a very real chance that you will forever be better off as a result of this experience."

CHAPTER 18

Feeling More Feelings

After talking to Dr. Dan, I relaxed, and I did something I don't believe I've ever done: I consciously tried to feel my emotions, using the RISEN framework to deal with them as they came up.

It was so…weird. I feel embarrassed saying this, but I don't even think I knew how to feel my emotions.

I had always pushed them away, or pushed them down, or mostly, distracted myself. I had no idea how much Netflix I watched, how much time I spent on Facebook and Twitter, or the hours of video games I played until this week.

I started paying attention to what I would do when an emotion came up, and I was always moving to a distraction. Once I saw this, I couldn't unsee it:

My whole life was distractions.

Without distractions, I found myself mired in my emotions, and it was—quite frankly—overwhelming.

Feeling my emotions was a whole new world, and I was like a baby in it.

* * *

Anne and I decided to have dinner a few days later. I was finally ready to talk about this with someone other than my therapist and Dr. Dan.

Alex: "You going to tell me what I can expect next? Because this has been some wild shit so far, and your description of it was...not the full story."

Anne laughed.

Anne: "I don't think it's possible to share the full story ahead of time. You kinda have to experience it."

Alex: "Isn't that the truth? I don't even know how to explain what I went through."

Anne: "Yeah, I don't usually share much about my experience, except with people who know me well or who know the work. People who haven't done it—they just can't get it.

"You know what's funny? So many people at the office noticed how much happier and more successful I was after this therapy. Lots of them asked how I did it. And I told them. Do you know you're the *only* one who actually followed up on my offer to connect with Dr. Dan?"

Alex: "I thought lots of people asked to be connected."

Anne: "They did. Probably a dozen people, at least. None followed up but you."

Alex: "Really?"

Anne: "You'll see this in your life. People will notice the changes, ask how you did it, and expect you to talk about a new diet plan or something. You'll say, 'Therapy,' and then nine out of ten will check right out.

"And even the one that's interested won't follow up. In over a year of people asking me, you're the only one from work who went through with it."

Alex: "I had no idea."

Anne: "You should be proud. You have real courage. Most people are too scared to take this step."

Alex: "Why?"

Anne: "You don't know why?"

Alex: "Well, yeah, they're afraid. But still, I was afraid. I almost didn't do it. But I did. Doesn't everyone else want to get better?"

Anne: "You'd think so. But no. I've come to realize that *most people prefer the pain they know to the joy they don't.*"

Alex: "I haven't been having much joy recently."

We both laughed at that.

Alex: "You never told me how hard this was. You just showed up happy one day and talked about how much better you felt."

Anne: "I did talk about my pain before, but it was just jokes about anxiety and memes about hiding my emotions and being dead inside. You know why those are funny, right?"

Alex: "Because they're funny, that's why! Explaining the joke kills it!"

Anne: "Alex, they're funny because they're true. That's how we both felt, and that's how we talked about it with each other— through humor."

I'd never thought about it like that, but she was right.

Anne: "But if I came to you with my pain before, would you even have understood how to talk to me about it? And why do you assume *I* even knew how to talk about it?"

Alex: "I guess you're right. I can barely even talk about mine right now. You aren't going to believe what my week has been like."

I told her everything about my session and then my conversation with Dr. Kate.

Alex: "This whole thing is kinda nuts to me, to think I have trauma?"

Anne: "I know, I went through a similar reaction. We're always raised to think our parents are basically good and do a great job, and we don't have any problems, or if we do, it's because we're bad kids. But that's not exactly true, is it?"

Alex: "I guess not."

Anne: "On the other hand, even if they did do a terrible job as parents, playing the victim and blaming them doesn't help either. *We have to both recognize we suffered trauma, but then also take complete responsibility for dealing with it.* It's exhausting when you first get it."

Alex: "And confusing. Does it ever get clearer?"

Anne: "Of course. The first session was probably the most confusing. The second session was the hardest, in terms of going deep and doing work. And the third gave me so much clarity and tied up so many loose ends."

Alex: "So, what do you know now that you wish you knew at the beginning?"

Anne: "That the whole point of this is to feel your feelings. *As I understand it, trauma is basically unfelt feelings. To heal your trauma, you must feel those feelings, and then you can let them go, and move on.* That was big for me.

'Trauma is basically unfelt feelings'—that sums up everything Dr. Kate told me in a sentence.

Alex: "This connection between trauma and feelings is so weird, isn't it? Why does no one talk about this?"

Anne: "I don't think anyone knows. Think about it this way: if you tried to convince fish that water was all around them, they'd think you were crazy. It's so pervasive, they can't even see it.

"I feel like trauma is the same way in our society. It's everywhere. Everyone was raised like this, so no one can see it."

Alex: "What if I feel like my trauma isn't that substantive? So many people had it worse than me, you know?"

Anne: "So, what if they did? My therapist helped me see that our traumas expand to fill the space in us."

Alex "What do you mean?"

Anne "Whatever problems we had, they feel the same to us as other people's problems feel to them.

"Imagine someone who grew up an orphan in the poorest place in America. They basically feel the same about their issues as we feel about ours.

"And the person who grew up rich, with everything, they had problems too, and to them, their problems feel as intense as ours feel to us. Whatever trauma we had, whether it was a lot or a little, feels about the same.

"My therapist explained it to me like this: trauma isn't a contest or a comparison. We're all climbing our own mountains, and the size of your mountain or where you are on it has nothing to do with the size of anyone else's mountain or where they are on it. All you can do is climb your own mountain."

Alex: "The thing that also messes me up is that stuff about my parents. I feel terrible that I think like they weren't good parents."

Anne: "That's the other thing I wish I knew ahead of time: *it's okay to see your parents as flawed.*

"In fact, they may have been far, far worse than flawed. They may have completely denied your reality and traumatized you—and thought they were loving you as they did it."

Alex: "What do you mean?"

Anne: "Most of the people we know have parents who are traumatized and stuck in their own stuff, just like us, right?"

Alex: "Yeah, that's pretty obvious now."

Anne: "Why do you think it was any different for our parents? They were kids once, and our grandparents were their parents. Where do you think our parents learned all of this?"

Alex: "No, my grandparents are amazing."

Anne: "Maybe they are, but every old person seems sweet. But they were young parents at some point. You think they were the same at thirty as they were at eighty?"

Alex: "I'd never thought of it like that."

Anne: "My therapist had me read this book, and one specific quote from it stood out so vividly. Hold on, let me pull it up; I put it on my Instagram."

"The way we were treated as small children is the way we treat ourselves the rest of our lives: with cruelty or with tenderness and

protection. We often impose our most agonizing suffering upon ourselves and, later, on our children."

—ALICE MILLER

Fuuuuuck.

I don't know why, but that hit me hard on so many levels.

CHAPTER 19

Some Family History

That Sunday I went to see my pa and granny for dinner.

Pa Bill and Granny Jane lived on a fifty-acre ranch about an hour outside town. I always took Murph with me, and she always knew where we were going as soon as we turned onto the highway and she caught the smell. She started squeaking and freaking out and was inconsolably happy and excited for the rest of the ride.

By the time we got there, Murph had slobbered all over the windows and was trying to climb out the one-inch window crack, she was so excited.

I opened the door, and she sprang out like a bullet, flew to the big oak in the front yard to chase the squirrels up the trunk. Then, she bolted down to the ponds to chase the ducks, then off to bark at cows and chase rabbits.

Pa Bill and Granny Jane came out to greet me and gave me big hugs.

Granny: "Alex, you look great!"

Pa: "Oh, kid, you look fantastic. Your eyes have a different light in them. Come on in, let's eat. We'll talk about everything after dinner."

I never ate on days I went to Granny and Pa's place because they cooked so much, and it was so good, I wanted to make sure I was starving when I got there. We had cornbread, roasted quail, beans, butter from their ranch, and all the iconic country dishes that Granny makes that I love.

After dinner, we sat in the living room and drank some beer.

Pa: "Okay, kid, enough of the bullshit small talk. I want to hear all about it. Every detail, let's have it."

I told them everything. The session, my thoughts afterward, the days I took off from work, my integration sessions with Dr. Kate and Dr. Dan—all of it.

Pa: "That's something else. Man, how the world has changed."

Granny: "I'm just so proud of you, Alex. You seem so much happier and lighter."

Alex: "I don't feel that way all the time, but thanks."

Pa: "Dr. Kate is right about all that trauma stuff. I've read some of Peter Levine's work, and it matches everything I've seen in my life. Both out here on the ranch with animals and in combat in Vietnam."

Alex: "You know about Peter Levine?"

Pa: "Like I said kid, I have friends who've been through this. You'd be shocked at how much my veteran friends know about trauma. We talk about this at the VFW all the time. One of the guys there became a psychologist after he served; he really got us into it, and now it's just a normal thing we talk about."

Alex: "So, what do you think about all the stuff with my parents? You talked about that some last time, but it feels hard for me to accept."

Pa: "Why?"

Alex: "I dunno. I just feel like so many people had it worse."

Pa: "Hell yeah, they did. Lots of people had it way worse. So what?"

Alex: "If they had it worse, like, how can I complain?"

Pa: "That doesn't make a shit-bit of sense, kid. The only person who's allowed to talk about having bad parents is the person who had it the very worst? If you didn't have the worst parents, you just have to shut up? How's that make sense?

"Could you imagine if I told one of my war buddies that his war stories aren't okay to tell because other guys had it worse?"

Alex: "I hadn't thought of it like that."

Pa: "We have so many of the guys at the VFW who barely saw action or a lot of the younger ones who were in the Iraq or Afghan wars; shit, half of 'em only drove trucks and maybe heard gunshots in the background or maybe saw a roadside bomb once. But we treat them as full vets, just like the guys who were on the front lines holding their buddies' guts in as they died. A vet is a vet.

"Yeah, of course, the ones who saw more action get more respect in a sense, but no one ever puts down anyone else's stories as long as they're true. Everyone's war stories are theirs, and we respect that."

Alex: "Man, I hadn't thought about that at all."

Pa: "You're thirty, kid; you haven't thought about a lot."

I laughed and threw a coaster at him.

Alex: "Another thing is: I feel bad about having trauma in a way. Like, it's disrespectful to my parents or something."

Pa: "Oh, to hell with that. We all have to accept our mistakes. And you did have shitty parents, kid. And guess what: I was a shitty parent to your mom too."

Granny: "Bill, now, that's enough."

Pa: "No, let's lay it out. Alex, you know me as this old guy who loves you and accepts you no matter what. And I am. But your granny and I weren't always like that. We used to be wild, and your mom grew up in that."

Alex: "What do you mean?"

Pa looked at Granny. She was getting misty-eyed but just nodded her head at him, like she was giving him permission.

Pa: "Let me tell you a story:

"Your granny and I met in high school, as you know. We fell in love right quick and got married right after high school. We both grew up real poor, and me especially—I came from a rough place. Granny had it better but not much better. We don't need to get into the details, but neither of us had families we wanted to spend a lot of time with, let's put it that way.

"We got married and moved here to start a new life. But as we found, you can't just leave your past behind. It comes with you. We were young, and we didn't really know what to do, so we drank a lot and even did some drugs. Mostly, cheap pot. We were poor too, so we lived around some shady characters, and they weren't the best influence, so basically, our lives became drinking and drugs and working, and that was it.

"Then, your Granny got pregnant with your mom, and we cleaned up for a while. But after the baby came, things got worse. We were young and stupid and had no idea how to take care of a baby. We both got back to some heavy drinking.

"It came to a head one day when your mom was about four. She'd been terrible, crying all day, and I'd been hitting the Jack Daniel's bottle pretty heavy, and your granny and I were arguing about something, probably being late on rent or how she was out of cigarettes or something like that. Then, we heard some banging around outside. Your granny was convinced it was a robber. I assumed it was one of our dumbass neighbors coming over to get a beer.

"So, I went out there in my tighty-whities and called out:

"'Jim, that you? We ain't got no damn beer!'

"No one answered.

"Then, we heard more banging, and your granny—who had been drinking too—got all afraid and told me it was a robber."

Granny: "Don't you put this on me, Bill! I did no such thing!"

Pa: "We've had a disagreement over this next part for decades. I contend she told me it was a robber and that I had to go see. She says I did it myself.

"*Whatever* the case, I got my shotgun and went out there.

"The banging kept going on, and when I flipped the lid off the garbage can, a damn raccoon jumped out at me, screeching and hollering.

"It clawed at my face, bit me, and then the real kicker: the damn thing wrestled my shotgun away from me.

"Your granny heard the banging from the trash cans get worse and me screaming, so she came out there shooting in the air with her pistol like Annie Oakley. It scared the racoon off."

Granny: "I found your grandpa on the ground, scratches all over his face and arms, bleeding like a stuck pig. And no shotgun."

Pa: "That raccoon stole my damn shotgun and dragged it off in the woods. We never saw it again."

Granny: "It was after that, I put my foot down. No more

hard alcohol, and we were going to find God and get our lives right."

Pa: "The next day, I got rabies shots. Then, we went straight to the church, introduced ourselves to the pastor, and said we'd like to find God; could he help us?

"He took one look at me and brought me to his study. We talked. We still go to that church, and I'm a rector there, as you know. Later on, after the military, that pastor helped me get a job on a construction crew, and I ended up running that crew, then starting my own company. But you know all of that part of the story.

"Jesus, son, close your mouth; you're gonna catch flies."

I didn't realize I was slack-jawed.

Alex: "Hold on, hold on, hold on. Let me get this straight:

"You two were white trash drunks until a raccoon wrestled a shotgun away from you, so you found God and turned your lives around?"

Granny looked at Pa with still-misty eyes, and he looked back at her...and she smiled.

I cracked up laughing.

I laughed like I'd never laughed in my life. A deep and profound laugh that came from someplace in me I hadn't known existed. I was crying and barely able to breathe, I was laughing so hard.

Then, Granny started laughing.

Granny: "Oh, Bill, you have to laugh; it *is* kinda funny!"

Alex: "KINDA FUNNY?! This is the funniest thing I've ever heard in my life!"

Pa started cracking up and laughing too, and all of us were both laughing and crying at once.

Alex: "How have you not told me this before?!"

Pa: "Hell, son, this is embarrassing! I own a business! I'm an important man in the church! I can't be blabbing about this nonsense."

Through fits of laughter, I tried to get more details.

Alex: "You were drunk in your tighty-whities trying to fight a raccoon?!"

Pa: "The damn thing won too!"

Alex: "It stole your shotgun from you?!"

Pa: "I never found it either!"

Granny: "Alex, he must have looked in the woods for weeks."

I can't remember how long we laughed about this, but it felt like hours.

Pa: "That was the clearest message I ever got from God, I tell you what."

Alex: "The only way God could give you a clearer message would be to set a bush on fire in front of you and speak out of it."

This was possibly the most joyous and cathartic moment I've ever had with my grandparents. They'd always been loving to me, but this was the first time I'd ever seen my pa actually be vulnerable and laugh at himself.

Growing up, he'd been this powerful titan of a man with huge hands and a deep voice. He ruled over our family like a king. He owned a big construction company, was rich and important and powerful. Larger than life. Yet he'd also been a white trash drunk who lost a wrestling match to a raccoon.

After we laughed until we couldn't laugh about it anymore, Pa got back to the point.

Pa: "Now that you know the real history, the other thing you got to think about is that your mom grew up in that trailer park with us acting like that. We didn't move out of there until she was five or six.

"And then I went from being a drunk, negligent dad to being a very strict disciplinarian father. I'm in my seventies now, and your mom is in her fifties. Looking back now, with forty-five, plus, years of hindsight, I can see I was probably too hard on her after that.

"Right after we moved to a nicer neighborhood, I was gone a lot because I'd just joined the military. I told myself it was about providing for my family, but maybe it was also about proving that I belonged and that I could make money and do something with my life. I don't know."

Granny: "Bill, you did the best you knew how."

Pa: "Yeah, I couldn't see it at the time, and I've only recently even begun to understand it, but I think I really hurt her. I don't think I've ever really accepted that."

Alex: "I had no idea about any of this."

Granny: "We never really talked about it. Not even with the kids. We didn't come from that generation. Where we grew up, you just didn't talk about your problems."

It reminded me of what Anne said about trauma being everywhere, but no one even seeing it.

Pa: "I've tried to talk about this with your mom, but she gets really angry, and it never works. We just can't seem to get past this."

Granny: "She has a lot of anger in her, that's for sure. And I can't blame her. I just try to love her."

Pa: "That's why I was telling you: you had a much harder childhood than you realize. I think your Dr. Kate might be right. I hadn't thought much about trauma as it relates to children, I'd only thought about it in terms of war, but everything she said makes total sense. You were alone a lot as a kid. Your mom had a real hard time when you were young. Do you remember your dad being around at all?"

Alex: "Not really. I only have a few memories of them together, and those are of them fighting."

Pa: "Yeah, that's about all they did once you were born."

Granny: "Don't make it sound like it's his fault, Bill!"

Pa: "I'm not. It's just what happened."

Oh fuck. I'd never thought about that…but it's true. Did I cause my parents to get divorced?

Pa: "That's why you spent so much time with us as a little kid: because your mom couldn't handle you and her own issues at the same time. It had nothing to do with you at all. She was just not handling it well. So, we did what we could, and we kept you as much as was necessary."

Granny: "You were a wonderful baby, and we loved having you."

Pa: "You were also a loud little monster, who got into damn near everything…but yeah, I loved you, of course."

As I drove home, I had so much to think about. So many things I'd never considered about my life.

My mom had a really bad childhood? *I* had a hard childhood?

For some reason, I kept coming back to something Dr. Dan had said, about finding my 'why' for this medicine.

My 'why' before had been helping myself.

But maybe there was a bigger 'why' now.

Maybe it extended to my whole family.

CHAPTER 20

Therapy Session: Taking Responsibility for Life

I went back to Dr. Kate the next week, my head spinning.

Dr. Kate: "How have you been feeling?"

Alex: "I've got a lot to fill you in on."

I told her the story that Pa Bill and Granny Jane told me. Then, I told her about what my pa admitted to—that he wasn't a very good father.

Dr. Kate: "Your grandfather sounds quite remarkable. That's not common for someone his age to do that."

Alex: "Do what?"

Dr. Kate: "Attempt to come to terms with his cruelty as a parent."

Alex: "Cruelty? Hold on now. How was he cruel? He was just absent. And strict."

Dr. Kate: "Of course. When I say, 'cruel,' I don't mean it in the sense that he beat her or anything like that. It's a psychological term that has a specific meaning: he did not recognize, allow, or validate your mother's childhood emotions.

"I'm not criticizing him. From your story, he saw that, admitted it, and even made an attempt to rectify it. I was commenting that it was remarkable he's doing that. Very few parents—of any age—do that."

Something about her comment bristled me. I couldn't figure out what it was, but I felt a distinct uneasiness with what she said.

Dr. Kate: "What's coming up for you when we talk about this?"

Alex: "I think I'm upset. This is weird. I think I feel something, but I don't know what I'm feeling or why."

Dr. Kate: "This is a big shift for you, to recognize emotions before you react. Would you like to explore it?"

Alex: "I guess so."

Dr. Kate: "Let me walk you through the way I see your grandfather, and you can tell me what you are hearing.

"From the story you told, it's pretty clear your grandfather grew up in a rough environment. It seems as though he was raised around alcoholism, violence, and despair and at a minimum, experienced neglect and physical abuse—and possibly a lot more."

Alex: "How would you know that? You're guessing."

Dr. Kate: "Not really. I'm making some assumptions but based on the evidence."

Alex: "What do you mean?"

Dr. Kate: "Let's see. I remember you telling me a while ago he had a job at ten and was working full-time at a logging camp at fifteen, right?"

Alex: "Yeah."

Dr. Kate: "Logging is a grown man's job, and very dangerous. Doing that so young means he was both very physically formidable and extremely tough and almost certainly in a home situation that was, at best, unpleasant. Fifteen-year-olds don't usually get that tough that quickly being raised around loving parents, and they definitely don't work at logging camps. At least not in the twentieth century.

"You told me a while ago that he barely finished high school and only graduated because your granny insisted that he have a high school degree to marry her. That tells me he had no encouragement or support at his home or from his parents.

"You also told me that he doesn't talk about his childhood. Everything you know about it, your granny has told you. That's a major tell for childhood trauma. People tend to share good memories.

"I also find it telling that he talks to you about his war experiences in Vietnam—which by all accounts were fairly intense—but not his childhood. That tells me he's either blocked out his childhood because it was so unpleasant or that his time in war had more valuable experiences than his childhood—connection with friends, a sense of adventure, some semblance of importance—or all of those things.

"The fact that he was often drunk for a period of his life tells me a few things: he suffered a lot of trauma as a child, he was not taught any way to cope with it, and the only effective outlet he saw around him was alcohol.

"The fact that he found God and redeemed himself, but then became a very strict and overbearing father, also suggests to me that he may have experienced physical abuse as a kid. Domineering, abusive parents, especially fathers, are almost all victims of physical abuse. That is the script they know, so to speak."

Alex: "The script? My pa was a way better parent than he got! And he was great to me!"

Dr. Kate: "He definitely was. On both counts. He sounds like an amazing man."

Alex: "Then, why are you criticizing him?"

Dr. Kate: "I don't feel as if I'm criticizing him at all."

I thought about it. She was right—she wasn't.

Alex: "I guess you aren't, but it feels like you are."

Dr. Kate: "Parents can definitely give more to their kids than they got from their own parents. And to his immense credit, it sounds like your pa gave your mom much more than he got. It appears to me that he gave you even more than he gave your mom. He grew over the course of his life and seems to still be growing. As I said, he seems to be a remarkable man.

"My experience has taught me this fundamental truth: *parents can ultimately only give their kids the same level of love, acknowledgement, and caring that they give to themselves.*"

Oh fuck. I felt like I was going to throw up. I pulled out my phone, flipped through it until I found the quote on Anne's Instagram feed and shared it with Dr. Kate.

"The way we were treated as small children is the way we treat ourselves the rest of our lives: with cruelty or with tenderness and protection. We often impose our most agonizing suffering upon ourselves and, later, on our children."

—ALICE MILLER

Dr Kate: "Oh yes, that's a famous Alice Miller quote."

Alex: "You know who that is?"

Dr. Kate: "Of course. She's a titan of psychology. Her books changed my life. I read the book that quote is from, *The Drama of the Gifted Child,* as an undergrad."

Alex: "I thought she was some internet guru or something. I guess that's why I couldn't find her to follow on Instagram."

I don't think I've ever seen Dr. Kate laugh that much.

Dr. Kate: "She was a Polish Jew who barely escaped the Holocaust as a child during World War II. She became a psychoanalyst in

Switzerland but then broke from that field and wrote several books about childhood.

"Her basic thesis is very simple and seems obvious to many people now but was revolutionary at the time:

"Most parents traumatize their children, completely unintentionally, mainly because they were traumatized by their parents, and the outlet to relieve their own pain is by doing the same thing to their kids. If they were humiliated as children, then they humiliate their kids, for example."

I sat and stared down at the carpet for a minute. I don't know why, but I felt like a wave of emotion hit me all at once. But I couldn't tell what emotions or where they were coming from.

Alex: "I feel overwhelmed right now. I don't know why."

Dr. Kate: "I can imagine. Sit with it for a moment. Perhaps a few pieces of the puzzle just clicked in?"

Alex: "What do you mean?"

Dr. Kate: "What do you think I mean?"

Alex: "Dr. Kate, I have no idea. I feel like I'm going crazy here. Can you stop playing psychologist for a minute, and tell me what's going on?"

She sighed and gave me the look you give to a little kid who dropped their ice cream on the playground. Compassion maybe?

Dr. Kate: "What exactly would you like to know?"

Alex: "I feel overwhelmed right now, and I don't know why. Maybe start there?"

Dr. Kate: "I cannot tell you why you feel the way you feel. I can make some guesses though, based on this conversation and on our history together."

Alex: "That would be amazing. Please do."

Dr. Kate: "It seems to me that you're waking up to some hard realities in your life. That overwhelms most people."

Alex: "What do you mean?"

Dr. Kate: "Okay, let's see:

"You decided to do MDMA because you felt unhappy and stuck.

"Your session unlocked a lot of emotions inside of you, waiting to come up.

"You initially thought you were the problem but then learned about trauma and how it works. You began to consider that you'd experienced trauma as a child, mainly at the hands of your mother.

"Then, your grandparents, who you love and revere, told you they traumatized your mother—obviously not on purpose, but they were not the caregivers to your mom that they were to you, which was news to you.

"Then, a big piece came into view. You realized that your grandparents were traumatized by their parents, and they had no tools to deal with this, so they accidentally traumatized your mother. She had no tools to deal with this, and so your mother traumatized you.

"And here you sit, waking up to the reality that not only have you experienced a lot of trauma in your life, but there are generations of trauma flowing down onto you from your family."

Alex: "That's exactly it! I feel like...I'm standing at the bottom of an avalanche of emotional shit!"

Dr. Kate: "That would me as well. In fact, it did."

Alex: "What do you mean, 'it did'?"

Dr. Kate sighed and gave me a long look. Like she was evaluating me.

Dr. Kate: "I generally don't like to share my personal life with my patients. I think it's a distraction and doesn't serve them.

"*But*, in rare cases, where my experiences might help to inform them on theirs, I'll do it. I believe this is one of those cases.

"Would you like to hear why I became a psychologist? It might help you understand what you're feeling right now."

Holy shit! In all this time, Dr. Kate has never once told me anything about her. Asking her questions was like trying to break a hardened criminal: she never folded!

Alex: "Please."

Dr. Kate: "When I was in college, I was a lost, sad, depressed girl. I thought everything bad in my world was my fault. I was bookish, focused totally on my studies, always got As, always did everyone's work for them in group projects and then resented them. I was also shy, never went to parties, followed all the rules."

Alex: "Oh, of course, I know that type."

Dr. Kate: "I read *The Drama of the Gifted Child* for an elective, and it shook my world to the core. I struggled to read the book because every sentence forced me to think about it for an hour before I could read the next sentence.

"It was like Alice Miller had been in my house and seen my childhood. *She was the first person I ever felt saw me,* and that feeling was something I'd never experienced before. It was miraculous.

"I probably read that book ten times in a row that semester. I dropped out of pre-med, much to the chagrin of my mother, and eventually dedicated my life to helping people through psychology."

Alex: "That's amazing."

Dr. Kate: "I'm telling you this because I think you're having a similar set of realizations."

Alex: "So, what else does Alice Miller say?"

Dr. Kate: "As a general rule, I like my patients to read primary sources for themselves and not rely on my interpretation. I'm an expert in my field, yes, but I believe people should take full responsibility for their own education and their own healing and not rely on anyone else to adjudicate meaning for them."

Alex: "I'll read her book, I promise. But can you catch me up?"

Dr. Kate: "The core thesis of her work is that parents who were traumatized project their repressed and unresolved emotions, feelings, and dreams upon their children. They unconsciously try to heal themselves by doing to their kids what was done to them: neglecting, ignoring, or worse—hurting, humiliating, and using them to fulfill their own emotional needs."

I thought about it for a second, and a memory popped into my head.

Alex: "You mean, like, if a dad always wanted to make the Majors but didn't, so he pushes his kid into baseball? Those are the angry dads at the Little League games, always yelling and going crazy, aren't they?"

Dr. Kate: "Yes, that's exactly right. Let me explain these theories through the lens of my life; it will make it easier for you to understand them, and you can see if any of them apply to you and your life.

"My mother and father divorced when I was young, and then it was my mother and I alone. My mother was very emotionally immature. She cared for my physical health and safety, of course, and from the outside, she looked like a normal mom.

"But she never really made a solid emotional connection with me. I was a desperately lonely child. I even went through a phase where I was an existentialist and thought this feeling was existential loneliness. It was not. My mother never once connected with me emotionally, and being that I was a child, I assumed it was my fault.

"Don't get me wrong, my mom fulfilled her role as mother in the ways she thought she was supposed to—she made my lunches, she went to PTA meetings, she dressed me up in pretty things, all of that.

"But all of that was all about her—how it made her look, how it made her feel. She never once asked or cared about what I wanted. In fact, she ignored me the times I would tell her my wishes or desires.

"I learned that I could not tell her things. I could not express my true emotions to her. Anything I told her, she viewed through the lens of how it made her look and feel."

Alex: "What do you mean?"

Dr. Kate: "If I told her I felt sad, she would take it as me criticizing her as a parent. Her response to my sadness was not to listen to it or help me sort it out. Her response would be to deny it or push it away, so she could feel she was a good parent by having a child who was never sad. Does that make sense?"

Alex: "Oh yeah. That hits home."

Dr. Kate: "This implicitly told me that my feelings and opinions had no value, only hers did. My mother made no attempt to know me, only to judge me in relation to her and her wishes."

Alex: "Wow. I had no idea your childhood was like that."

Dr. Kate: "Alex, everyone has a story, and until we get to know the person, we have no idea what that story is."

Alex: "Yeah, that's so true."

Dr. Kate: "Let me back up a step and give you some general background on child development. I'll try to make this as non-technical as possible.

"A child needs unconditional love and acceptance to thrive. A parent must give that to the child and, ideally, expect nothing in return. That's what makes a parent/child relationship so unique among all other relationships a person will have in their life.

"And to really accept a child, a parent must love and accept the child, whatever they do, not only when they smile charmingly but also when they cry and scream. The best thing parents can do for their child is to love them for *who they are*, not what they do.

"To get to a place of loving them for who they are, they have to be emotionally attuned to them. They must notice their children's moods and welcome their feelings with interest. They help their children understand their emotions, instead of rejecting or shaming them for emotions the parent does not like or cannot handle. They help their children see that it's okay to feel and talk about any emotion that comes up.

"This enables the child to experience their feelings—sadness, despair, the need for help, for example—without fear of making the parent insecure. They know they are able to express their wants freely because they will be loved by the parent no matter what.

"By creating this space, an emotionally mature parent helps their child feel grounded and safe, so that they grow into healthy adults.

"In order for a parent to do this for a child, they must themselves have developed confidence, self-awareness, and comfort with their own feelings, as well the feelings of others.

"Does this make sense so far?"

Alex: "Yeah, but I don't know any parents like this. I guess my grandparents were kind of like that."

Dr. Kate: "Yes, in your case, I would say I just described your grandparents. They fit that description fairly well.

"Many parents are not like this. They are emotionally immature. They're so preoccupied with themselves and their own traumas that they don't notice their children's inner experiences.

"These parents are uncomfortable with their own emotional needs and, as a result, have no idea how to support a child at an emotional level. They cannot tolerate the wild emotional swings or emotional expressiveness of a child. These parents may even have extreme reactions to emotional outbursts from their children, getting nervous or angry at their children, punishing them instead of comforting them.

"They reject some, or all, of the emotions a child feels—unless those emotions align with what the parent wants. This rejection of their emotions shuts down a child's instinctive urge to connect with their caregivers, leaving the child feeling alone and disconnected.

"This sort of emotional loneliness is so distressing to most children that they will do anything to avoid it and try anything to make a connection with the parent.

"Basically, they will intuitively understand that their parents are using them for this purpose and become so attuned to her parents' expectations that they do whatever it takes to fulfill the emotional needs and expectations of their parents, while ignoring their own feelings and needs."

Alex: "This sounds bad."

Dr. Kate: "It can be, yes. It gets deeper though.

"The child will also shield their parents—and themselves—from the truth about the negligent parenting they have received, even idealizing their parents and striving painfully to earn their approval. They will, in essence, become a 'perfect' child for their parents.

"By doing this, the child loses their true self. By becoming the 'ideal child,' the child loses their true feelings and identity.

"This denial begins as a survival mechanism for a child when they're young. They cannot fully feel, let alone express, even the most basic emotions such as discontent, anger, rage, pain, even hunger—for fear that their parents won't love them."

Alex: "Fuck. That is me."

Dr. Kate: "It seems so."

Alex: "But...this is so cruel. Why would someone do this to a child?"

Dr. Kate: "They don't know they're doing it. Everything they do is either about imitating their parents or unconsciously finding a way to alleviate their own suffering. Very rarely is this done on purpose or with knowledge."

Alex: "Can you give me an example?"

Dr. Kate: "I'll give you an example from my life. I came from a Jewish family, with a deep emphasis on education. My mother was obsessed with me getting good grades and doing well in school and going to a good college. It was drilled into my head from as early as I can remember. My mother's love for me felt to me based on my grades and performance in school.

"And then one day, in college, I decided I'd had enough. I wanted to drop out."

Alex: "What? Don't you have a PhD?"

Dr. Kate: "I do now. But then, I went to her, and I told her I was dropping out, and she got very, very upset. I was a pretty logical arguer even then, and this was after I'd read almost everything Alice Miller had written at that time, so I was not going to give in to her anymore.

"For every argument she made, I had a solid counterargument. I pointed out the holes time and again, until, finally, exasperated, she screamed at me:

"'What will my friends think? What will people say? My daughter can't drop out of an Ivy League school! I'll be a laughing stock!'

"And everything became clear in an instant: Alice Miller was right."

Alex: "She said that?"

Dr. Kate: "Oh yes. It was both exasperating and liberating, all at once. I was heartbroken because part of me still thought this wasn't true. But it was also freeing because I was able to let her go and become my true self. I didn't speak to her for many years after that."

Alex: "But you stayed in school?"

Dr. Kate: "Yes and no. I realized that dropping out was my way of getting back at her. If I was dropping out to spite her, that was not fundamentally different than staying in to please her. Just the other side of the same coin.

"So, instead, I took what people now call a 'gap year,' and I traveled all over the world. I found out who I really was, what I really wanted, and my purpose in life.

"I decided to return to school and dedicate myself to psychology, specifically to helping people work through these issues."

Alex: "That's amazing."

Dr. Kate: "It is now. It was very hard to go through at the time."

Alex: "Do you talk to your mom anymore?"

Dr. Kate: "I think I've told you enough. I will tell you this last part because, again, I think it's relevant to you: yes, I do.

"We ended up mending our differences, to an extent, years later. It took a long time and a lot of work—she made some major changes in her life, as did I—but in our case, it was doable. It does not always work that way, but in my case, it did."

Alex: "How? What created the change?"

Dr. Kate: "There isn't a short answer to that question. The shortest answer I can give is this:

"First, I forgave her because I realized that she was only doing to me what her parents did to her.

"Second, she realized what she had done to me, took responsibility, did her work, and apologized."

Alex: "Wow, she apologized?"

Dr Kate: "Yes. But that was *many* years later. After she'd gone on her own healing journey."

I stopped and looked out the window, processing these bombshells.

Alex: "So, what you're saying is that most parents dump their shit on their kids, and those kids dump that shit on their kids, and this shit just keeps rolling downhill for generations."

Dr. Kate: "Yes. That's why I became a psychologist. To help people stop the 'shit avalanche,' as you call it.

"This is the point of the therapy we're doing. When you have emotionally worked through the history of your trauma and have regained your sense of being alive, we'll be done."

Alex: "This feels overwhelming."

Dr. Kate: "It can feel that way. But there is a good side: you can do this. It's very simple, actually."

Alex: "Simple? How?"

Dr. Kate: "Take full responsibility for it."

Alex: "Full responsibility? I didn't do this. I was a kid."

Dr. Kate: "You are absolutely right."

Alex: "It doesn't seem fair."

Dr. Kate: "Maybe not. Alex, I will tell you this:

"We don't get to pick our parents. Nor do we pick our childhood. But we do get to choose our response to them both, and we can only do this by taking full responsibility for our own lives.

"Ultimately, that is all we can do, but by doing that, we can have everything we want."

CHAPTER 21

Integration Session: "When do I do another session?"

Things felt pretty good over the next two weeks as I continued doing all my integration work:

1. Feeling and using RISEN to process
2. Breathing using pranayama
3. Journaling
4. Meditating (not well yet)
5. Taking long walks with Murph
6. Doing talk therapy with Dr. Kate

I set up an appointment with Dr. Dan. I filled him in on everything I'd gone through and all my realizations about me and my family.

Dr. Dan: "That's great work. Let's take a step back for a second. You're doing an amazing job feeling in ways that you've never known how to feel before.

"I also want to reflect to you how much you've done in a relatively short period of time. Not only are you feeling more, you're actually starting to understand why it's there.

"You're being present with your pain, continuing to move through it, continuing to talk it out, continuing to make context and narrative of it, but not at the expense of the feeling itself.

"You're actually bringing the feeling closer, so you can get to know it and hear what it has to teach you. This is really good work."

Alex: "I feel like I might be ready to do another session, so I wanted to talk to you about that. How do I know if I'm ready?"

Dr. Dan: "It sounds like you're asking the right questions. You're looking at it as another opportunity to learn and grow and open, as opposed to wanting to get rescued or fixed. That's always a healthy approach and intention. It sounds like you've got a good degree of readiness."

Alex: "Will this be as hard as the first one?"

Dr. Dan: "Hard to predict. It's doubtful that it will be exactly like the first one because no two experiences are the same. It has the opportunity to be easier because you've unpacked a lot already.

"It also has the opportunity to be more challenging because now you might have an easier time building expectations and think that the process that's going to be ahead is just like the process that just happened."

Alex: "So, you're saying it's going to really suck?"

Dr. Dan laughed in that way he does: with his head back and eyes all squinted.

Dr. Dan: "Possibly, yes. But remember, your last session had a lot of good parts as well."

Alex: "Like the love? Yeah, that's true. The other day, out of nowhere, I got really angry. Like a lot. What's that about? I couldn't even tell where it came from."

Dr. Dan: "Oftentimes, anger is a protection from other emotions, like grief or sadness. You feel anger because it pushes away sadness. So, if you're angry, that could be a good sign. It means you're feeling. The next step would be to get in touch with sadness and, ultimately, grief.

"I'm curious: do you have any idea what that's about for you specifically?"

Alex: "Well, I've been talking about this with my therapist. I think the sadness goes back to—for the most part, it goes back to the stuff with my parents and my childhood.

"I guess this is part of grief. I have to recognize that my childhood wasn't what I thought it was, and in fact, it was pretty bad for me in some ways. So, I'm sad about it, I guess?"

Dr. Dan: "Yeah, it can be related to the ways that you didn't get the love and support you really wanted and needed as a child."

Alex: "I still have a hard time getting past the idea that other people had it way worse."

Dr. Dan: "Yes, other people have it way worse, but if you judge the validity of your sadness based on not experiencing the degree of trauma others felt, you're demeaning your emotional experience. *You don't have to experience massive trauma in order for your pain or grief to be valid.*"

It was getting easier but still such a hard thought to bear—that my pain was valid. But I couldn't understand why.

Alex: "What about my fear and nervousness around the next session? Part of me feels like I need to do it, and part of me is afraid. What do I do with that?"

Dr. Dan: "That's understandable and totally natural, and I think it can be helpful too because fear often is an indication that something big is happening.

"Remember though: fear and excitement are actually the same physiological response. I mean that literally—a fearful body and an excited body are having the same sympathetic nervous system response."

Alex: "Wait, really?"

Dr. Dan: "Yep. These two responses involve the same chemicals. Fear is just excitement with a negative frame. And excitement is fear with a positive frame. You get to choose how you frame the emotional response. But they are literally the same adrenaline, norepinephrine, and cortisol responses. Think of it this way: do you like riding roller coasters?"

Alex: "Yeah, I guess so. They can be fun."

Dr. Dan: "You know how some people pay hundreds of dollars and wait hours in line to ride them, while others don't go on for all the money in the world?"

Alex: "Right."

Dr. Dan: "The physical response is the exact same in the two types of people. The excited people are leaning into it and accepting—even enjoying—it. The fearful people are running from it and letting it overwhelm them. But their bodies are having the same reaction."

Alex: "That's crazy."

Dr. Dan: "Yeah, I remember learning this in medical school and not believing it. I had to look at the primary sources myself, but it's true."

Alex: "Is there anything I need to do between now and the session for prep?"

Dr. Dan: "Rest. Get good sleep. Take care of yourself. Practice your breathing exercises. Meditate. Be light; have fun. Come into it with your most excited, open, available self."

Alex: "Yeah, yeah, I know your answer—if I do my integration work, it'll all work out."

I had to say, "Yes." I had to go back in.

CHAPTER 22

Medicine Session 2: Courage to Surrender

I got even more serious about my integration practice and my preparation for my next session.

I practiced my breathing twice a day, on schedule. I floated in the deprivation tank once a week. I even tried to meditate each day. It was terrible, and I hated it—it seemed like my mind would immediately flood with crazy and disjointed thoughts—but I sat down, and I attempted it. And in one session, I even felt like I had a weird flash of enlightenment and peace. It left almost as soon as it came, but it gave me a lot of encouragement. If I got there once, I could get there again.

I read some of the books Dr. Kate mentioned. One of the quotes that punched me the most in the gut came from *The Body Keeps the Score*:

"One does not have to be a combat soldier, or visit a refugee camp in Syria or the Congo to encounter trauma. Trauma happens to us, our friends, our families, and our neighbors."

This guy is, like, the world expert on trauma, and here is saying something that I never would have thought to be true. I also listened to some of the podcasts Dr. Dan referred me to and, man—it was all really eye-opening. I learned so much about my life, and I was still shocked that no one ever really talks about it.

I journaled every day. I recalled so many memories from my past I'd forgotten or dismissed and re-examined them with my new understanding of myself. The more I wrote, the deeper I was able to go.

I spent my sessions with Dr. Kate diving deep into what I'd written about and what I was feeling, trying to understand where it was coming from, then letting myself experience the feelings.

It was like I had a new relationship with reality. And all sorts of emotions were coming up that I'd never explored before.

I fully accepted that I did have trauma in my life, and whether it was or wasn't that bad didn't really matter—it's what happened, and I started to accept how it had affected me.

And I got serious about preparing for the next MDMA session.

I found an eye mask that fit me perfectly. I switched my outfit to basketball shorts and a polyester blend T-shirt—as much as I sweated in the last session, this would help me stay comfortable.

I focused more on my preparation as well. I realized that last time I'd been full of anxiety and resistance.

But this time I wasn't. Because I'd done this before, I felt I could release all the jitters and uncertainty and focus on what mattered: feeling my feelings.

There was a flip-side to it though: I felt a lot more dread.

It's hard to describe, but I felt like there was something deep and dark in me that was bubbling below the surface, waiting to come out. You know that feeling you have, the one where you're waiting for the other shoe to drop? That's how I felt.

I decided to stay with my emotions and my feelings and surrender to whatever comes up.

The day of the session I woke up about fifteen minutes before my alarm, which was better than last time, when I woke up three hours early.

I got to the clinic, walked in, said, "Hi" to the receptionist, and went back to my session room, where Dr. Naomi was setting up.

Dr. Naomi: "Hey, Alex, how are you feeling?"

Alex: "Great, actually. This feels like a totally different experience than the first time. Nowhere near as anxious."

Dr. Naomi: "Yeah, that happens with some people. Once you've gone in and you know what it's like, you can relax and focus on the work more."

I took my GABA and laid back, starting my breathing practice.

Dr. Dan came in about thirty minutes later with the MDMA.

Dr. Dan: "Great to see you, Alex. How are you feeling today?"

Alex: "Great. I mean, given that I'm about to dive into emotions I've spent my life avoiding."

Dr. Dan: "Good to hear. Your first dose is in front of you; you can take it whenever you're ready."

I popped it in, swallowed it down, put the eye mask on, and went in.

As I waited for the medicine to kick in, a rush of anxiety hit me. I became convinced that the medicine was not working, and that I got a faulty batch, and I was doing it wrong, and last time was a fluke.

All these thoughts flooded my head, like a wave of anxiety crashing over me, all at once.

Alex: "Are you guys there?"

Dr. Dan: "Yes."

Alex: "How long has it been since I took the medicine?"

Dr. Dan: "Let me see…twelve minutes."

Alex: "Are you sure this is MDMA? Like, maybe you picked up the aspirin instead? It happens, man; I wouldn't be mad."

Dr. Dan: "Yes. We have very strict protocols in place to ensure the patient gets the right medicine, at the right dose, at the right time."

Alex: "Is it possible it's stopped working for me?"

Dr. Dan: "I doubt it. But maybe let's give it some time and see. It usually takes forty-five minutes, at least."

Alex: "Why do I feel this overwhelming anxiety?"

Dr. Dan: "This is pretty common, especially in the period before the medicine hits."

Alex: "I didn't feel this way last time."

Dr. Dan: "Each journey is its own experience. What are you feeling?"

Alex: "Like the medicine isn't working, that nothing is going to happen, that this is a huge waste of time, that nothing will come up. I don't know—stuff like that."

Dr. Dan: "This is a very common feeling before the MDMA takes effect, even the second time. Would you like to practice breathing together?"

We did the breathing technique, and it worked. I felt better and was able to relax into the session more.

I'm not sure how long it took, but it snuck up on me and hit me all at once. That incredible feeling of love and serenity and warmth and joy came over me. It was not quite as intense as the first time, but it was still amazing.

I felt the body high come on, same as last time. The deep relaxation, the release at my core of everything that I didn't even realize I was holding onto. It all came on, building slowly.

I let my mind wander and found myself crying but not tied to a specific memory.

Alex: "Why do I always cry on this stuff? I don't really cry anywhere else. And I feel sad. I think."

Dr. Dan: "For many people, MDMA brings up emotions they have trouble accessing without it. Perhaps, ask yourself: 'what could I be sad about?'"

I thought about that for a while. And then, I decided to take his suggestion literally and said:

Alex: "Alex, what are you sad about?"

Before I could think about a response, I started bawling. I cried and cried and cried.

Alex: "Where is this grief coming from?"

Dr. Dan: "Maybe we can explore it later. What if you gave yourself permission to feel it right now?"

Alex: "I'm scared though. I can feel something coming. It feels big. What do I do?"

Dr. Naomi put her hand on my ankle and spoke in the calmest, most caring voice.

Dr. Naomi: "Remember, Alex, we're here with you. Nothing can hurt you that's outside of you. All the events coming up have already happened. You survived them. This is about feeling and processing your emotions around them. You can trust us to protect you."

Oh fuck. That's so right. I forgot about that—I already survived whatever it is I'm afraid of. All I need to do now is feel the emotions.

For some reason, that gave me a lot of courage. If it already happened, then I could endure the memory of it. It wasn't like I was having to do something new that was risky.

I decided to do what worked last time: surrender to it. Whatever needed to come up, I would let it come up.

And man, did it come. I cried like I've never cried in my life. Deep, heaving sobs wracked my whole body. I'm not sure, but it felt like I was even wailing at one point. Like the way you see in the movies where a mom sees her kid die or something, that sort of primal wailing? That's how it felt.

It almost felt like I wasn't even involved in it, like I was simply a witness to what my body was releasing. I had no idea where this deep reservoir of sadness was funneling up from; it must be a place in me I didn't even know existed.

The most confusing thing is the emotional release didn't seem tied to an event, at least not that I could tell. It was just pure emotion.

Alex: "Why don't I have a memory associated with this? Why is it just the emotion?"

Dr. Dan: "There are several potential reasons. We can talk about that afterwards. For now, perhaps, let yourself feel this. This is the work."

So, I felt. For what seemed like hours.

I had no idea how long the actual time was because when I was on MDMA, I lost all sense of time. I'd think it had been ten minutes, but it had actually been two hours, or vice versa.

As the intensity of the emotion tapered off, I started to see events in my mind's eye: things in the past, memories, stuff like that.

At first, it was happy memories. All of them were me with my grandparents.

Me, sitting in front of the TV, watching college football with pa, eating Doritos and drinking cranberry juice, which I used to crave as a kid—and, really, what a weird flavor combination.

Me and Granny, gardening and playing with the bugs we found outside.

Me and Pa, getting my haircut and talking to all his friends at the barbershop.

Me and Granny, cuddling in her bed at night, as she read to me.

Then, the sad memories came. And they involved my mom and dad. Mostly my mom, which makes sense; my parents divorced when I was little, and my dad wasn't around much.

I did remember the time I was five and I accidentally broke a bottle of beer my dad was drinking. He yelled at me and was really mean. I remember thinking, "Why is he so upset about this? There's more beer in the fridge."

The time I was six and my mom didn't pick me up from school. I was alone for hours at a bus stop.

When I was seven and my mom stormed on the field during a soccer game and screamed at a ref, and I was mortified.

The time I was nine and my mom gave my dog away and didn't even tell me until I got home from school.

There was scene after scene like this. It was like…the worst movie I could imagine.

So many of the events were small. Little things my mom did that I don't think I realized were so painful at the time.

Times she ignored me.

Or yelled at me.

Or called me a name.

Or put me down in a small way.

Or said what I did wasn't good enough.

It was weird. If one of these things had been in there by itself, I'm not sure I would have noticed or paid attention. But the medicine kept showing me these things over and over.

I never thought of myself as someone who avoided my emotions, but now I could see pretty clearly I was. I avoided them a lot.

And I had no idea these things had such an effect on me.

I had no idea there were so many.

I had no idea they hurt me so much.

As I sat and went through painful event after painful event in my life, I realized something, deep in my soul:

I'd suffered a lot of trauma.

And I cried about it.

CHAPTER 23

Therapy Session: "That's why I love *Harry Potter* so much?"

I scheduled my next session with Dr. Kate to come right on the heels of the medicine session. I wanted to talk to her when I was as raw and open as I could be.

I started by filling her in on the details.

Alex: "You were right. My parents traumatized me. And I felt it."

Dr. Kate: "It sounds like you had a very intense session."

Alex: "Yep."

Dr. Kate: "Where are you now?"

Alex: "I don't know. It feels really bad, honestly. But also, kind of cathartic. Like I just had the biggest poop of my life."

Dr. Kate: "I've never heard MDMA therapy described that way. But let's go deeper. What do you feel now?"

Alex: "I feel like my parents were pretty awful to me in ways I'd never considered or felt. It was almost like…like I saw the same events in my life I already knew about, but this time, I saw them from a different angle. It was like someone took the same facts and told a new story about them, one I wasn't allowed to tell before."

Dr. Kate: "What story is that?"

That stumped me. I sat there dumbfounded for a second, but just like during the session, a voice in the back of my head spoke up almost without me thinking it.

Alex: "I don't know. That my parents didn't love me?"

Dr. Kate: "That sounds accurate to me."

Alex: "You're saying my parents didn't really love me?"

Dr. Kate: "What was your experience with them like? For you, I mean?"

Something about the way she asked that question struck me. She didn't ask me what they did or even what I felt…she asked about my experience with them.

I sat with that for a second and really thought about the word "experience." From my gut, with incredible force, I felt the words come out of my mouth almost before I thought them.

Alex: "I never experienced love from my mom or dad."

She looked at me in that way she does, without judgment or anticipation or anything.

I started crying again.

Alex: "I mean, yeah, my mom told me she loved me. But I never felt it. Her words didn't mean anything to me because I never experienced any love behind them. They were just words."

I cried some more.

Alex: "What does this mean? That she didn't love me?"

Dr. Kate: "I don't know what she felt. It's not my place to judge that. And honestly, Alex—I don't care. I only care what you felt. That's what we're here to discuss: what you felt, not what she felt."

Alex: "What do you mean?"

Dr. Kate: "It's not helpful to try and figure out whether she loved you or not. We can if you want, but it doesn't matter. Her whole existence might have revolved around her love for you, or she might not have had an ounce of love in her for anyone. It doesn't matter either way.

"What matters is how you experienced her. If you didn't experience love, that's the reality we're dealing with, and you must take responsibility for it."

Alex: "Dr. Kate, I have to say, this is such a mindfuck—how can her intention not matter? I mean, if she loved me and I didn't feel it, doesn't that say something about me?"

Dr. Kate: "Maybe. But let's stick with this hypothesis for a little while. For you, what matters is your *experience* of her."

Alex: "How could that be?"

Dr. Kate: "**Because emotions are facts.** What you felt is a fact. Our job here is to help you recognize what you felt, and then help you feel it fully, so you can let it go, and then move on with your life.

"Remember our conversation about trauma? Right now, you're stuck with this trauma and can't move forward in your life until you've felt these emotions and processed them."

Alex: "Yeah, I remember that, but you gotta help me understand this more. I'm still wondering if she loved me or not."

Dr. Kate: "Let's assume the best: she did love you. And your dad. Let's even assume they'd both pass a lie detector saying that they love you.

"It still doesn't matter. Because your mind still experienced a reality where, regardless of how much they loved you, *you did not experience that love, and that was traumatizing to you as a child.*"

Alex: "I'm struggling with this. It doesn't matter if they loved me?"

Dr. Kate: "Whether your parents loved you or not—whether

they were good parents or bad parents—isn't the question. We're not here to judge your parents. We're here to deal with your emotions.

"The only question that matters is what emotions you have to deal with.

"Once you understand that, you can let go of the judgment around that question and just deal with your feelings as they are."

Alex: "Let go of whether they were good or bad parents? Like, not even consider the question?"

Dr. Kate: "Nope. We can talk about whether they met your needs, of course. That's the more important question. But whether they were 'good' or 'bad' is just a judgment, and it doesn't help you.

"This is why I don't judge what your mom did. I focus on what you experienced instead. Have you noticed that?"

Alex: "Yeah."

Dr. Kate: "That's because the facts that matter for this work are your emotions. You had needs as a child—to be seen, to be heard, to be loved, to be accepted as you are—and you did not experience your parents as meeting them, and that created a wound in you, and that is the reality we are dealing with."

Alex: "I've never heard anyone talk about it like this."

Dr. Kate: "This is fairly well-established in many fields of psychology, but yes, you are right—most people do not think or talk in terms of needs. They talk in terms of blame and judgment. That's almost never helpful."

Alex: "So, all that matters is what I experienced and felt."

Dr. Kate: "If we're talking about your trauma, then yes. If we're talking about your relationship with your mother, then it's slightly different: her needs matter in your relationship as well. But she isn't here, and this isn't about her or your relationship with her. This is only about you and what you experienced."

I thought about this for a long time. Maybe two minutes. And something really profound hit me.

Alex: "My god, you're totally right. That's why I love *Harry Potter* so much. It's because I always felt like the kid under the stairs."

Dr. Kate: "Excuse me?"

Alex: "You know the *Harry Potter* books, right?"

Dr. Kate: "Of course. I read them to my kids when they were young."

Alex: "Okay, I *loved* those books."

Dr. Kate: "Tell me why they seem to land so deeply for you."

Alex: "Most people love the wizardry, or the magic, or the Quidditch, or whatever. And that stuff is cool. But you know what parts I would read over and over again? The beginnings. Where Harry was still living with his Muggle extended family."

Dr. Kate: "Tell me more."

Alex: "Okay, you know how almost all the books begin, right? He's living with his aunt and uncle and his crappy cousin. And they treat him terrible, right? For god's sake, they make him live under the stairs like he's some kind of indentured servant!"

Dr. Kate: "Oh yeah."

Alex: "I would read those sections again and again. It was the very first time someone had identified *how I experienced my life as a kid!*

"I felt unloved. I felt unwanted. I felt like my emotions were not important. I felt like I was lied to and manipulated. I felt held back. And now I understand *why* I identified so much with those scenes.

"*I felt like Harry Potter: unloved and uncared for, living under the stairs.* Obviously, my mom didn't do that exactly, but that's how I *felt*."

Dr. Kate: "Because that's how you experienced your childhood."

Alex: "Right! Now I get what I was seeing in my last session. I was seeing all the examples of this. All the times I felt unloved as a kid."

Dr. Kate: "It makes sense."

Alex: "Those parts of the book were my life reflected back on me. For the first time, I felt my experience was validated. It was like when you read Alice Miller for the first time."

Dr. Kate: "That is very insightful."

Alex: "Holy shit. Now I get everything the MDMA was showing me. It was showing me the specific times I felt that way. It felt like there were *hundreds* of them. It was like a movie of abuse."

I thought about it for a minute.

Alex: "My god, Dr. Kate…she was a terrible fucking mom. She was awful."

I started to get angry. My tears were gone now, and there was something else replacing it. Rage? I was trembling.

Dr. Kate: "Put words to it, Alex. Put words to the feelings."

Alex: "Now I get it. Yes, I *was* treated like shit as a kid, and yes, I have denied that to myself because—just like Harry Potter's aunt and uncle—I was told that my parents were great!

"Mainly by my parents, but still, they continually told me that my perception of reality was wrong and that they were fantastic. She treated me like shit and told me she was awesome. What the FUCK!"

I actually got up and paced around Dr. Kate's office. I ranted and raved and yelled about my parents. I just let myself be angry for a while and feel the anger. I'll spare you the details; you can imagine it. I eventually calmed down and sat back down.

Alex: "It all makes sense right now. All the trauma stuff, and the Alice Miller stuff, and all of it. I was the gifted child, who could have done anything I wanted if someone would just listen to me and believe in me."

Dr. Kate: "You still can do anything you want."

Alex: "How?"

Dr. Kate: "Instead of relying on your parents to meet those needs, you can do it for yourself. Like I keep telling you, no matter who traumatized you are and no matter why they did it, it's still your responsibility to deal with it."

She's right. Goddamnit. It was like my anger got defused all at once. *How does she do this shit?*

Alex: "How do I deal with this?"

Dr. Kate: "First, let's explore your anger. This is a good sign. It's the next step. It's healthy to feel the anger inside of you before moving to the next step."

Alex: "Okay, I will. And then after anger?"

Dr. Kate: "You might not like what I'm going to tell you comes after anger."

Alex: "I just realized I'm Harry Potter; I can handle anything now. Give it to me, Dr. Kate!"

Dr. Kate: "The next step is forgiveness."

Alex: "Ohhhh…fuck all of this therapy bullshit!"

Dr. Kate: "Alex, I can tell that did not land well with you. That's fine. You're still angry, and we'll make all the space you need for your anger."

Alex: "You want me to FORGIVE THEM? After I just realized how awful they were?"

Dr. Kate: "Not now. When you're ready. It may take a while."

Alex: "How am I supposed to forgive them?"

Dr. Kate: "Listen very closely:

"I did not say to tell them they were right.

"I did not say to excuse them or their behavior.

"I did not say to validate them or their behavior.

"I did not say to let them back into your life.

"I did not say to accept this treatment again.

"I did not say to believe any lies.

"I only said that if you want to let this trauma go, you must accept your experience as real and valid, which you are doing.

"Then, you must allow yourself to feel whatever emotions come up, which right now is anger and where we should focus.

"Then—only when you have felt your anger and are ready to— can you take the next step and forgive them for what they did."

Alex: "Fine, I'll bite: why THE FUCK would I forgive them after everything they've done?"

Dr. Kate: "There's a long and complicated answer to that. Basically, it's so you can let go of any resentments towards them or pain you are holding onto and then move on with your life.

"Forgiveness is for you, not for them."

CHAPTER 24

"Why Can't This Just Be Easier?!"

I spent the next week feeling really, really angry.

My journal looked like a bomb went off in it: angry chicken scratches all over the place, wild accusations. Rage spilled all over the pages.

I didn't talk to anyone in my family, I just kept my anger to myself and my therapist. Dr Kate told me that feeling the anger was fine but that I might not want to discuss it with anyone I was angry with until I sorted through more of it.

Yes, I might still be angry at them later, but I would be able to discuss my anger calmly. That made sense.

I did talk to Anne about it (since I wasn't angry with her, of course).

Alex: "I'm so angry. How could she do that? How could my mom be such a terrible parent?"

Anne: "It's a hard realization. And unfair."

Alex: "And how could I not know until now?"

Anne: "It's crazy, isn't it? I felt the same thing: disbelief, then anger."

Alex: "I saw it and felt it so clearly. My parents took my childhood and used it for themselves! They didn't care about me at all."

Anne listened to me rage. I was so livid as I detailed all these memories of being let down and abandoned and left alone. Anne was so nice about it, just reflecting back on me and listening and really being great. I eventually wore myself out and sat back exhausted.

Alex: "This sucks. I mean, I know things will be better later, on the other side of this. I kinda wish I was there now."

Anne: "Have you thought about the story you're telling yourself? 'Things will be better later.' What if you saw them as better now?"

Alex: "What do you mean?"

Anne: "What if there was no later—but only right now? What if all there was were the feelings you had at this moment?"

Alex: "That would really suck if things are considered better now. This kinda sucks, Anne. I can't ever remember feeling this mad at anything."

Anne: "What if that's a good thing?"

Alex: "What do you mean? How could it be a good thing to be this mad?"

Anne: "The anger was there before. Isn't it better to be awake to the pain that was silently hurting you so much? To see and feel the truth?"

Alex: "What good is the truth though?"

Anne: "The truth is where all healing begins. To gain true self-confidence, you must know the truth of your own story. You aren't betraying your parents by seeing them accurately. Thinking about them objectively can't hurt them. Feeling the truth of your emotions, like anger, can't hurt them. But it can help you."

Alex: "Who the fuck are you, the Buddha?"

We laughed together, but she got right back to it.

Anne: "I'm serious. This anger was in you, wasn't it? You just ignored it and pushed it away and pretended it wasn't there. But it was. All this medicine did was help you uncover it and finally feel it, right?"

Alex: "Yeah, I guess."

Anne: "I prefer being awake to the truth. Even with the pain."

Alex: "This all just feels really heavy. I had a perfect delusion built before. From a certain angle, I had a great life, right? I have a cool job. I have a nice apartment. I have friends and stability and all of that. I had a great life."

Anne: "You started this whole process because you hated your life. You don't like your job. You live in a dull douche-cube. Your friends are people who are just as asleep as you were."

Alex: "Hey! You used to be one of us!"

Anne: "I know. And then I woke up."

Alex: "Ouch."

Anne: "I did this medicine because I had the life I thought I was supposed to want, and I hated it. Isn't that close to why you did this?"

Alex: "Yeah."

Anne: "And?"

Alex: "I felt like...I was at the top of a mountain before. Yeah, maybe it wasn't a great mountain, but I had climbed that mountain only to find out...it's the wrong mountain. And now, I don't know what to do."

Anne: "I had the same realization."

Alex: "What did you do?"

Anne: "I got angry, like you are. Spent a lot of time angry about a lot of things. And then I went down that mountain and began climbing the right mountain."

Alex: "That sounds like a lot of work."

Anne: "It is."

Alex: "I'm struggling with wanting it all done now. I am struggling with realizing that it's a journey. The more I see that, the more I find myself frustrated with myself."

Anne: "I get it."

Alex: "This morning, I was making eggs, and I wanted to turn up the heat to cook the eggs faster. But that doesn't work. High heat doesn't do the same thing faster. Great eggs just take time. I got so angry at the eggs, I threw them in the sink and didn't even eat them."

Anne: "Suffering is the price we pay for the joy of life. In this physical existence, you cannot have one without the other."

Alex: "Seriously, you sound like Dr. Dan now."

Anne: "He does kinda rub off on you, doesn't he?"

Alex: "In the most annoying but nice way, yeah, he does. I said the words 'hold space' to someone the other day."

Anne: "I totally mimic some of his phrases too. I now 'reflect back' on people all the time because of him."

We both laughed.

Alex: "I'm so fucking frustrated."

Anne: "What if you were kind and compassionate to yourself instead of hard on yourself? How much easier would it be for you?"

Alex: "That's hard for me to do."

Anne: "That's a story you're holding onto. You can change that story if you want."

Alex: "Yeah, I've gotta do that."

Anne: "Listen to that—your language is shame-based. 'I gotta let it go'—that's a demand on yourself. What if you were compassionate and kind to yourself as you struggle with the suffering of life and move through it?"

Alex: "I don't know. I hate how agitated I am all the time."

Anne: "Again, with the judgment. You said, 'I hate how agitated I am.' You're judging yourself. What if you accepted your emotions, and let them be for a while, just to see where they took you? Isn't that what Dr. Dan and your therapist tell you?"

Alex: "I get what you're saying, but that seems like a totally foreign idea. Being kind to myself? I don't want to lay around all day and watch Netflix."

Anne: "Alex, that's distracting yourself, not being kind to yourself. You know that."

Alex: "I don't know anything anymore. What does it even mean to be kind to yourself?"

Anne: "That was hard for me to learn. It's still hard in some ways. I'll tell you some things I realized:

"Doing this work was being kind to myself. I was finally taking my emotions seriously. Accepting that my emotions are valid and meaningful, no matter what they are. Being patient with myself and allowing my emotions to have their say, even if they were hard or threatening. Realizing that I get to decide what my life means, and what my story is, was a big one.

"And even simple things: taking time to journal, taking time to rest, taking time to eat right, taking time to work out—those are all forms of self-care.

"Or even more basic: feeling that I'm worthy of self-care and then setting boundaries around myself to make that happen. Before I started this work, I had no idea how little regard I had for myself or how poorly I treated myself and how badly I let other people treat me. It was shocking."

Alex: "How do you even start that? I feel like an idiot for asking how to take care of myself."

Anne: "I know, right! How shocking is it to realize that you don't really even know how to take care of yourself?

"My therapist gave me a really interesting analogy. He asked me how I would treat a million-dollar racehorse. And I love horses, so of course, I went into detail about all the things I would do: the food, the padding in the stall, and the muscle therapy, and all of that.

"Then, he asked me, 'Well, how much of the equivalent do you do for yourself?'

"The honest answer was none. I realized I treat animals better than I treat myself."

Alex: "I totally treat Murph better than I treat myself. She gets the best organic, locally-produced, grass-fed meat diet. We go on long walks every day. I take her to get groomed once a month at the place where they massage her and rub fancy oils into her hair. She loves it."

Anne: "Would you ever let anyone hurt Murph? Or even talk badly to her?"

Alex: "I dare a motherfucker to look sideways at her. I'd fucking kill 'em."

Anne: "What about you? Who defends you?"

Goddamnit. She was totally right. I didn't even have to say anything; Anne knew me too well.

Anne: "I know two people who have your back."

Alex: "My pa and granny?"

Anne: "Okay, I know four people."

Alex: "Who are the other two?"

Anne: "Dr. Kate and me. And Dr. Dan—that makes five."

Alex: "Man, don't make me fucking cry at this random taco place."

Anne: "You can also give yourself credit. The fact that you're doing this therapy and the integration is great. You *are* doing self-care. My therapist told me this too, and I really liked it:

"At its core, self-care is keeping promises to yourself."

Alex: "Man, that's deep."

Anne: "Then, let's celebrate a commitment you made is to yourself that you already followed through on: doing MDMA therapy. That's such a big deal, Alex!"

I smiled. She was right. I was being pretty hard on myself. Maybe I did deserve some credit for really committing to myself and then following through.

Alex: "Is this how you've killed it at work over the last year? Doing this therapy and focusing on self-care?"

Anne: "Pretty much. Once I started valuing myself and setting boundaries, the world just adjusted to accommodate it. It was the weirdest thing. Can I tell you something, though? To be honest, I don't think I'll be there much longer."

Alex: "Why not?"

Anne: "Once you start this journey, you realize what really matters. I can't find anything that actually matters at that job. Why stay? I think I have a different calling in life."

Alex: "What are you gonna do?"

Anne: "I have no idea. I need to sit with it more, but I'll find my path soon."

Alex: "Dr. Dan wasn't kidding when he said this process can really upend your life."

Anne: "Yeah. It was scary to me at first too. Like I said, I choose to focus on taking care of myself and being content in the moment, and it really works well. Keep going, you'll get there."

I sighed loudly and slumped in my chair.

Alex: "Ugh…why can't this just be easier!?!"

Anne: "If it was easier, we'd all be in heaven already."

CHAPTER 25

Integration Session: "How can I forgive?"

A few weeks later, I had my next integration session with Dr. Dan.

Alex: "Dr. Dan, I feel like I might be stuck. I'm trying to move past my anger, but I don't think I've forgiven my parents yet. How do I forgive them?"

Dr. Dan: "Do you want to?"

Alex: "I want to move past this, and when I talked with Dr. Kate, it seemed like forgiveness might be part of it."

Dr. Dan: "It could be."

Alex: "Not necessarily justification, none of that. Just forgiveness."

Dr. Dan: "Yeah, you don't have to agree with what they did. And it can be helpful to be in a place of forgiveness so that you don't have to hold on to the resentment."

Alex: "That's exactly what she said."

Dr. Dan: "Have you gotten a sense from Dr. Kate of where you're at in that process? Like, are you close, closer than you've ever been? Are you on trajectory for achieving that goal?"

Alex: "This is becoming clear for the first time in my life. This is something I need to do. And not just around my parents. The other weird dynamic is that I realized I have to forgive myself for a lot of things that I did wrong, mostly to myself. I feel like I've treated myself pretty poorly, and I feel a lot of shame about that. And a lot of guilt about it."

Dr. Dan: "Sounds like you've been doing amazing work, so let me take a second to reflect that back and continue to shower the kudos. Well done."

Alex: "Thanks, Dr. Dan."

Dr. Dan: "In my experience, one of the best ways to get to forgiveness is through compassion and understanding. And one of the best ways to have compassion and understanding is to really see it from the other person's perspective.

"How were your parents stuck in their own cycle of depression and confusion? How were they disconnected and in pain and ignorant about their impact on you? I like to try to even understand their upbringing, understand their childhoods, understand where they came from, where they were at in their own life at that moment."

Alex: "So, yeah, in both MDMA sessions I saw a lot of the dynamics with me and my parents. I still haven't brought it up with them, and I'm honestly not sure when I'm going to—I may or may not. I don't know."

Dr. Dan: "You don't have to know."

Alex: "I feel like it's probably best for me to work through my stuff first before I talk to them, and I'm not there yet. It'd be too raw. Dr. Kate says I'd be speaking from a wound instead of a scar, which makes sense.

"I want to try and get to a forgiveness point but, honestly, it's hard. It feels maybe I'm not through with my anger towards them."

Dr. Dan: "You may not be. I would caution to not get to forgiveness too fast. If you jump to forgiveness too quickly, without feeling all the underlying emotions, then what you are doing is effectively bypassing them. This is a way to repress the deeper emotions. That doesn't help you deal with them, and they will end up coming out and expressing in some other distorted way."

Alex: "Yeah, I've been pretty angry over the past month."

Dr. Dan: "Okay, that's great. I just want to put that out there, because I do see that a lot from patients—they will immediately forgive someone who wronged them, without actually letting the emotions come up. Which I would argue is not really forgiveness; it is simply pretending to forgive and moving on, but the underlying emotions are still there.

"This is a process. None of this is a light switch that's going to go on and stay on. This work requires a constant coming back to understanding, coming back to compassion and being with the feelings and working on them. You're still moving through that early material.

"It's important that you understand this is a constant reexam-ination process, not a fix-it-once-and-it's-done process. Do you understand that?"

Alex: "Yeah, I guess. That's not fun, to have to keep coming back to stuff though."

Dr. Dan: "It's not, but you aren't coming back to the same stuff. You're coming back to deeper layers of the issue."

Alex: "What does forgiveness even mean? Is it an action? Is it something I do? Or is it a place to get to? I'm confused about that."

Dr. Dan: "Forgiveness tends to be a practice that creates peace. If weight-lifting is a practice to get stronger—if yoga is a practice whose outcome is physical vitality and structural integrity—if prayer is a practice in order to get to union with your Creator, then forgiveness is a practice in order to get to peace and compassion.

"Forgiveness is like the sister of gratitude. They work closely, and they're quite interwoven. The more we are able to stay in gratitude, the easier it is for us to forgive the wrongdoings of others, so to speak."

Alex: "Okay, but *how* can I forgive them?"

Dr. Dan: "It's much easier to forgive people when you realize that whatever they've done wrong has been done out of igno-rance—not malice.

"Ask yourself: 'what was their childhood like?' Did they have models for parenting? What tools were they working with?"

Alex: "My pa told me that he wasn't a very good dad to my mom."

Dr. Dan: "Yeah, once I realized that in my life, things really opened things up for me. Once I learned to see my parents as flawed and incomplete, struggling with their own issues, then I could forgive them—without having to accept the parts of them or their behavior that did not meet my needs. There is a great quote about this from Alden Nowlan. I believe it goes like this:

"'The day the child realizes that all adults are imperfect, he becomes an adolescent; the day he forgives them, he becomes an adult; the day he forgives himself, he becomes wise.'"

I thought about this for a while. And all at once, it was like a bunch of pieces clicked into place.

Alex: "What about myself? How do I forgive myself?"

Dr. Dan: "What do you have to forgive yourself for?"

Alex: "I'm not sure. I guess for the way I treated myself?"

Dr. Dan: "What do you think you should've done differently?"

Alex: "I should have treated myself a lot better. With more respect. Maybe taken better care of myself?"

Dr. Dan: "What would that have looked like?"

Alex: "Paid attention to my needs, not abused myself so much with drinking or whatever. Maybe not so hard on myself. Listened to my emotions. Loved myself. Things like that."

Dr. Dan: "Why do you think you were that way to yourself?"

Alex: "I guess because I thought I deserved it. That would make sense, wouldn't it?"

Dr. Dan: "If there was a self-loathing or a self-punishing aspect, then that would be because you thought you deserved it."

Alex: "Is there another aspect to it?"

Dr. Dan: "Yeah, sometimes we're not taught differently, so we don't see the obvious other options. If we treat ourselves harshly, it might be because we're trying to be better in order to receive the love that we really needed.

"The inner dialogue goes something like, 'If I could just be more perfect or be the right son or the right daughter or the right partner, then at that point, I'll be worthy of receiving their acknowledgment.' So, it isn't necessarily self-punishing; it might be self-perfection.

"Or, if I'm hard on myself it might be because that's what I've been taught to do. You just beat yourself into betterment, because if you don't, then you will feel you're never going to be good enough."

Alex: "Because of the love you didn't get?"

Dr. Dan: "There's a lot of different ways that it spins itself out, but it usually comes down to a series of questions:

"Am I lovable?

"Is love safe?

"Am I worthy of receiving love?

"Not just am I lovable, but am I loved for who I am?

"Have I done enough to get love?

"If I get love, can I trust it?

"Does the world have my back?

"Is the world a safe place?

"If I have something, am I going to lose it because somebody is going to try and grab my shit?

"Do I have to continue to watch my back?

"From what you've told me, with your therapist, you're getting closer to these core issues: how you were not taught to love and, as a result, you had no reference to what self-love looked like, felt like, or how it was enacted."

Alex: "That sounds a lot like the Alice Miller stuff that Dr. Kate and I talked about."

Dr. Dan: "Oh yeah, it is. Alice Miller was a huge influence on me as well. Maybe ask yourself, 'what could I do on a daily basis that would be an example of self-love?' You weren't taught that, shown that, or given any context for it. So, maybe you're punishing yourself for something you had no way of knowing."

Alex: "That doesn't seem like a great idea, does it?"

Dr. Dan: "It's not the most effective way to treat yourself, no."

Alex: "You said before that the medicine is not going to do this work for me. What do you mean by that? Dr. Kate said something similar as well."

Dr. Dan: "If it's your work to get to a place of understanding deeply within yourself, you have to do that yourself. You must make the decision to do it, then do the work. The medicine is simply a tool that can help you open the space to make that work easier.

"To expand a common metaphor: The medicine doesn't give you a fish. It doesn't even teach you how to fish. It shows you that there are fish and points out where the fish are. The rest is up to you."

Alex: "Yeah, Dr. Kate keeps saying something similar, that I'm responsible for healing my trauma, regardless of where it came from. I fought that for a while, but I think she is right. It's my job now."

CHAPTER 26

Medicine Session 3: Facing the Darkness & Finding the Light

Alex: "Okay, let's do it."

I took my MDMA, put my eye mask on, and laid back.

Session three was underway.

I focused on my pranayama breathing and let my mind wander.

My last few weeks had been less intense, in terms of new revelations, but still very transformative.

I'd spent my sessions with Dr. Kate diving deeper into the trauma and parental abuse, feeling my anger and unpacking all the implications.

And wow—who'd ever think it was so hard to take care of yourself? I never realized how *bad* I treated myself until I actually looked at it. That whole thing about "no one can give more to their kids than they give to themselves" really shook me.

I want to have kids one day, and I want to be a great dad, but once I took a true inventory of how I really treated myself—how much I slept, how much I worked out, how much I did things I really enjoyed, how well I ate, how I organized my life—*I realized I treated myself like shit.*

In addition to all the integration work I was doing, I committed to my life in a way I'd never done before.

I started working out consistently, three times a week.

I got all the junk food out of my house. No processed sugars, no processed grains, no seed oils. Just healthy whole foods like meat and vegetables. Yeah, I had to go to the grocery store a few more times a week, but that's fine; I deserve it.

I started paying attention to my sleep hygiene, going to bed and waking up at consistent times and ensuring I got at least eight hours of sleep a night.

Nothing fancy. I stuck to the basics, and one by one, made some of the changes I'd always thought about but never did.

I realized something big—my life had played out very different than Dr. Kate's. Dr. Kate became her mom's little perfect daughter to get her love. I was far more rebellious and fought my mom a lot. I wasn't as concerned with my mom loving me. I was willing to be myself, at least to some degree. Yeah, I had a lot of the attributes of the "gifted child," but I also was missing quite a few as well.

I think maybe that's because I had something Dr. Kate did not: I had my grandparents there, loving me like emotionally-mature parents. They weren't a huge part of my life—I lived with my mom 95 percent of the time—but it was like that 5 percent was just enough to make sure I had a stable foundation. I always knew I had a place to go and people who loved me, at least on some level.

This all led me to realize how thankful I was. What would have happened to me without Pa Bill and Granny Jane? I owe them so much.

That's when I felt the warm tears on my cheek.

Alex: "Lemme guess. It's been forty-five minutes?"

Dr. Dan: "Forty-one minutes to be exact."

Alex: "Yep, I can feel it hitting me now. The tears are the tell for me. I think these are for appreciation."

Dr. Dan: "We'll be here, of course, but remember what we talked about: if you let it, the third session can be the most powerful and the most intense. It may bring some difficult emotions up, but if so, that's because it's what you need to heal."

I could feel the emotions bubbling up, like from deep down within me.

As they came up, I felt myself fighting them. Pushing them away. I felt like I was in physical pain.

Then I remembered my promise to myself: *I am going to sur-*

render to the medicine, I am going to let myself open up, and I am going to feel as much as I can feel.

And I did.

A wave of loneliness and terror swept over me.

I kept swinging back and forth between allowing myself to feel my emotions, then feeling overwhelmed and pushing them away. Going back into pain, then coming back and surrendering to it.

Finally, I remembered something I read. It was in the Alice Miller book. I put it on my Instagram page, and I read it every day for the past few weeks. I started reciting it to myself, out loud. I probably got the quote wrong, but this is what I said to myself:

Alex: *"Our access to our true self is only possible when we're no longer afraid of the intense emotions of early childhood. Once we've experienced this world, it's no longer strange and threatening. We no longer need to keep it hidden behind an illusion. We know who and what caused our pain, and it is exactly this knowledge that gives us freedom at last from the old pain."*

I refused to fight it anymore.

Alex: "Whatever happens, happens. I will surrender to the process and accept these emotions and let them come."

That worked because they came on. Pretty quick and pretty hard. I felt like I was dying. Like, I legit thought I would die.

But I stayed with them. I let myself go. *If it's my time, then so be it.*

And then, just like magic, all the hard emotions lifted. And in their place was the most serene, soulful, happy, content moment of my life.

Alex: "Is that it? I just have to let the emotions come, do their thing, and then they go on their own?"

Dr. Dan: "Pretty much."

Alex: "Fuck, man! I thought I was surrendering before, but I wasn't. Not really. I just tried it, and it was awful for a few minutes, and then boom, they're gone, and now it's like, everything is amazing."

Dr. Dan: "This is the perfect time to feel them then."

Alex: "Right, good idea."

I let myself float, and like last time, I felt these images come into my head.

The first thing I saw was my mom. I haven't talked to her in a long time. Maybe nine months? A year? We hadn't had a relationship really at all since I left for college over ten years ago.

The impression I kept getting, over and over, was that I needed to reach out to her.

I guess I was fighting it somewhat because this image stayed with me, letting me see this from different angles.

Alex: "Fine! Dr. Dan, can you write something down for me?"

Dr. Dan: "Of course."

Alex: "Write down that I need to call my mom."

Dr Dan: "Done."

As soon as I said it out loud, the image left and another one came up. I stayed with that a while, but it was an easy one.

Alex: "Dr. Dan, please write this down. I'll know what it means: Introduce Pa to Dr. Naomi."

Dr. Dan: "Done."

Alex: "Wait, I guess I should ask first: Dr. Naomi, are you down to be my pa's guide for his MDMA sessions?"

Dr. Naomi: "I'd be happy to talk to him, of course. If he's willing and a good candidate and we're a good fit for each other, of course, I would."

Alex: "Awesome. Sorry, Dr. Dan, I don't mean to cut you out, but I know my pa really well. He would think you're a soft leftie intellectual and wouldn't trust you enough to open up. I don't think that obviously, but he's from a different generation. He'll like Dr. Naomi, though; she has a similar energy to my granny. You good with that?"

Dr. Dan: "Of course, Alex, whatever is best for you and Pa, I'm happy with."

Alex: "This MDMA is like a truth serum, ain't it! I feel like I'm supposed to feel bad for telling you the truth, but I don't. I mean,

I'm not making a bad comment about you, obviously—you know that, right?"

Dr. Dan: "Of course. I don't mind at all. I got into this profession to help people, and that means meeting them where they are and accepting them for who they are."

As soon as I said it out loud to Dr. Dan, it floated away, and something else came into my head.

This was less of a set of questions and more of a direct message. It kept coming to me, and I tried to understand more deeply, but I couldn't do it. It confused me. But I called it out anyway.

Dr. Dan: "Can you write this down for me: 'ask Anne about her boyfriend.' I don't know what that means, but that's the message that won't leave my head."

It floated away as soon as I said it.

The next one was hard for me. I'll admit I fought it. I don't know why, but I fought it a lot. Then, I realized I was afraid. But then I felt like I had an option: go face my fear and then get the full message, or if I wasn't ready, to let it go until another time.

Man…it was messing with me. Come on, with a tease like that, I had to face the fear. I surrendered, and damn, was it brutal.

I felt a terror come over me. This was possibly the worst fear I've ever felt. And then the memories came with it:

Kids laughing at me after I screwed up a science project in third grade.

My fifth grade teacher telling me that I wasn't smart because I couldn't do fractions.

A high school teacher making a joke about how it's a good thing my grandfather owned a business, so I could get a job.

My mom criticizing me after I tried to start a lemonade stand as a kid and used her nice glasses for it.

My dad yelling at me that I couldn't do anything right after I broke his weed whacker.

Memory after memory like this of me failing at something, being mocked or shamed or emotionally castrated by people telling me where I fell short or what I couldn't do.

It was brutal. But I sat back, and I felt all of the emotions. I felt the heat of the shame. The cold of the loneliness. The gut-wrenching misery of being told I wasn't good enough.

I felt it all, and it all washed over me and then off of me.

I was drenched in a cold sweat by the time it was done, but I felt relieved, like I had just let go of a huge backpack of misery and fear.

CHAPTER 27

Therapy Session: Confronting Reality and Setting Boundaries

Alex: "Dr. Kate, I know I promised the medicine—or myself, or whatever—that I would reach out to my mom...but I don't want to."

Dr. Kate: "You don't have to. Everything in life is a choice."

Alex: "Why you gotta say it like that?"

Dr. Kate: "Say it like what?"

Alex: "You're making me feel guilty."

Dr. Kate: "You may feel guilty, but I don't make you feel anything."

Alex: "Ugh, you and the 'responsibility for your emotions' thing again."

We both laughed. This was an inside joke with us. I'd put emotions that I didn't want to accept on her; she'd remind me that I'm responsible for my emotions, and no one can make me feel anything, etc.

It's called projection. She taught me how it works a long time ago, and she's totally right. It shocked me how much I did it once I started to see it.

Alex: "Okay, I feel guilty, and of course, that's on me."

Dr. Kate: "What do you feel guilty about?"

Alex: "I made a promise. I don't know who or what I made it to, but I made it. But damn…I really don't want to."

Dr. Kate: "Let's explore that. Why not?"

Alex: "I don't know."

Dr. Kate let me sit there in my non-answer. I used to always say 'I don't know,' and she would point out that this was a way to not only avoid emotions but try to get her to help me understand them. It was probably a tactic I developed as a kid, and I was pulling it into adulthood, but it wasn't serving me anymore. So, every time I said that, she'd just sit and wait for me to explore my feelings and figure it out.

She could wait out a meditating monk. I knew I would break first. So, I didn't fight it; I let the next thing come up.

Alex: "I guess I don't want to talk to her."

Dr. Kate: "Mmmmm."

Alex: "I don't like talking to her."

Dr. Kate: "Okay. Can you access why you feel that way?"

Alex: "I don't know…I guess I don't like the way she makes me feel."

Dr. Kate: "She's in control of your feelings?"

Alex: "Okay, I know she's not in control of my feelings. Lemme rephrase: I don't like the way I feel when I talk to her."

Dr. Kate: "That's very different. You know why I always come back to that, right?"

Alex: "I get it intellectually."

I then started to channel her language, teasing her a bit.

Alex: "*Placing the locus of control for my emotions into someone else gives them power over me and my emotions, and it denies my autonomy and power over my life. It creates a victim mindset in me.*"

Then, I shifted back to my voice.

Alex: "I totally get that, and I agree. I've even gotten pretty good at it in most areas of my life. But this is a tough one. It's my mom."

Dr. Kate: "Exactly—and that's why it's the most important place to really see it and deal with it. As a child, you can reasonably say that your parents are in control of your emotions to some extent but not as an adult. At that point, everything you do is a choice, but you can only change it if you see it."

Alex: "Were you like this with your mom? When you broke from her?"

Dr. Kate: "Oh yes. Remember how I told you I decided not to drop out? The reason was because I knew I was dropping out solely to spite my mom. That's no different than staying in to make her happy—I was letting her dictate my decisions.

"Taking the year off gave me the space to discover myself, examine my own wants and needs, and answer the question about why I was in school to begin with. I wanted to make my decision to stay or go based on my *needs*, and not based on my mother's *wants* or as a reaction to her.

"It was the first time in my life I owned my emotions and made a decision solely based on what I needed and wanted. But it was very hard to do. It took me almost a year to make that decision."

Alex: "Where'd you go on your year off? You have some crazy adventures?"

She gave me her "no games" face.

Dr. Kate: "That's definitely not a session topic. It's both a distraction from you and not relevant to the issue at hand."

Alex: "Okay, fine."

I don't know why, but this whole line of conversation made me feel much better.

In my eyes, Dr. Kate is like a paragon of strength and courage and steadiness. To know she used to be an insecure book nerd in college, had to fight her mom to become a psychologist, and dropped out of school for a year not only made her human, but helped me realize that people don't step out of the womb like her. They make themselves into successes.

I knew this, but it was different when I saw it and felt it.

Alex: "I feel like all this stuff with my mom is a massive anchor on me, weighing me down and tying me up. I know my mom was doing what she felt she needed to do for me, I guess. In a way, I even feel sorry for my mom. But I also feel a lot of anger. And maybe even…hatred? I don't know. It's very confusing."

Dr. Kate: "Tell me more."

I sat and thought about it for a second, and that little voice in the back of my head told me to tell the truth—to myself. The words sprung from my mouth.

Alex: "I'm worried if I talk to her, then I have to have compassion for her, which means I have to forgive her. Then, I have to let her back into my life."

Where did that come from?

But damn, it was right. I felt immediately lighter.

Dr. Kate: "That's understandable."

Alex: "Do I have to?"

Dr. Kate: "What do you think?"

Alex: "No?"

Dr. Kate: "Is that a question?"

Alex: "No. It's not. I don't."

Dr. Kate: "And?"

Alex: "How do I do it? How do I talk to her without all that stuff I'm afraid of happening?

Dr. Kate: "What do you think you might say to her?"

Alex: "'Hey, Mom, I did a bunch of drugs, and they told me to call you'?"

Dr. Kate actually laughed at that.

Dr. Kate: "That would be quite amusing, but I'm not sure she'd get the joke."

Alex: "Yeah. I honestly don't know what I'd say. I don't know."

More poker face from Dr. Kate. *Ugh.* Do they teach this in psychologist school? This woman could stare down the final table in the World Series of Poker, I swear.

Alex: "Fine. I guess I would say something like, 'Hey mom, haven't talked to you in a long time, wanted to reach out.'"

Dr. Kate: "Okay. Then what?

I felt myself go blank. The white space feeling again.

Alex: "I honestly don't know. I'm not even sure what I'd want out of reconnecting with her."

Dr. Kate: "That's a great point. What might you get?"

Alex: "I don't know. I can't see us having a relationship."

Dr. Kate: "Why not?"

Alex: "I guess it's possible. I just...I can't see my mom changing."

Dr. Kate: "Would you have guessed your pa was considering doing MDMA-assisted psychotherapy six months ago?"

Alex: "No chance."

Dr. Kate: "So, what might you want from this? Let me be clear: I don't have an agenda here except you and your wellbeing. I'm not pushing for you to reach out to her or not. I think you should do what you believe is best for you right now in your healing process."

Alex: "What would you do if you were me?"

Dr. Kate: "I'm not you; I can't answer that."

Alex: "Okay, what did you do when you were faced with the prospect of reaching back out to your mom? How did you handle that?"

Dr. Kate: "Honestly...I didn't want to do it."

Alex: "Why?"

Dr. Kate: "This comes back to what I told you a few sessions ago: forgiveness.

I knew part of me would be stuck in that relationship until I addressed it. I decided I would reach out, I would make an attempt to have a relationship with her—but only on my terms and in a healthy, positive way. And if that didn't work, then I was willing to let her go."

Alex: "That makes total sense. But what does that have to do with forgiveness?"

Dr. Kate: "In order to be at a place where I could reach out, I had to have compassion and understanding for her and her mistakes as a mother and be willing to forgive her for those.

Once I realized that my mother was the way she was because her mother treated her that way and that she did the best she could, given the tools and the courage she had, then I saw her actions as coming from a place of ignorance and not malice.

I was able to see her as who she was: sad, depressed, lonely, and hurt and using her relationship with me to try and make herself feel better. None of this did she understand as she was doing it. It was just what was done to her, and she imitated it."

Alex: "Yeah, but you faced your stuff and did your work! She didn't!"

Dr. Kate: "You're right. She didn't. Though she did apologize, in her own way. And I forgave her before she'd done that anyway."

Alex: "How? Why?"

Dr. Kate: "Because holding onto my anger only hurt me."

Alex: "But you were right! She was wrong!"

Dr. Kate: *"Do you want to be right, or do you want to be happy?"*

Fuuuuuuuck.

Alex: "Can't I be both?"

Dr. Kate: "Not in this case. Because in this case, 'being right' is a defense you are using to hold on to your—very justifiable—anger at your mom."

Alex: "I don't get it."

Dr. Kate: "Being right means you get to be angry. But being angry only hurts you.

"There's a famous Buddhist quote about this: 'Holding onto anger is like drinking poison and expecting the other person to die.'

"I realized that was true for me and my anger towards my mom, so I decided to let go of my anger."

I didn't know what to say. I still felt very angry and upset. I wanted to yell at Dr. Kate. I wanted to scream curses at her, actually. Which made no sense.

Alex: "I'm really angry right now, Dr. Kate."

Dr. Kate: "I can imagine. Alex, I chose to be right for a long time. It made me angry and miserable. Then, I chose to let go of that anger, and I became quite content and peaceful."

Alex: "How'd you do that?"

Dr. Kate: "I forgave my mom."

Alex: "Really?"

Dr. Kate: "There's a common thread through all the ancient spiritual teachings regarding one's enemies. Jesus was particularly known for his teaching here, and I think he's the greatest historical example of this. You went to church, right?"

Alex: "I still do sometimes with my pa and granny."

Dr. Kate: "His primary teaching, the one that made him stand out, is what?"

Alex: "Love your enemies."

Dr. Kate: "Exactly. Most people don't really understand what he meant by that. At worst, they see it as pacifism. It was not at all. Jesus was a fighter, in his own spiritual way. At best, they see it as forgiveness of sins. Which it is. But it's even deeper than that.

"Jesus had a very sophisticated understanding of human psychology. He knew that if you hold anger towards another, that you are the one bearing the cost of that emotion. I believe he stated it as such:

"Don't judge, and you will not be judged. For in the same way that you judge people, you yourself will be judged."

Alex: "Dr. Kate, I had no idea you knew your Bible!"

Dr. Kate: "Like I told you, I was a book nerd."

Alex: "I'll do you one better. Peter asked Jesus how many times he should forgive his brother or sister who sinned against him. Jesus said, 'I tell you, not seven times, but seventy-seven times.'

"That always bothered me, because I thought Jesus was saying to accept people treating you bad. A turn-the-other-cheek thing."

Dr. Kate: "But he isn't. What he is saying is to let go of your anger towards others by forgiving them. Another way to say it is that when we cling to anger, we are clinging to what separates us from our own happiness.

"Letting go of this anger means not only releasing the person who has wronged us but releasing *ourselves* from the anger and making space for ourselves and our joy. This opens up a place inside of us that we can fill with love, instead of anger."

Alex: "How are we supposed to love someone who treats us badly? Because the preachers could never really answer that question to my satisfaction."

Dr. Kate: "I'm not a biblical scholar, so I won't speak about what Jesus says on this. But I do understand people, so make no mistake: I'm not telling you to accept abuse from people. Ever.

"Let me explain what I did. It may help you.

"I didn't immediately let my mom back into my life.

"I had to first recognize and accept my emotional needs.

"Then, I had to draw very clear boundaries with myself about what I would and would not accept from my mom and from others.

"Then, I communicated these needs and boundaries to my mom and enforced them.

"Had she not respected those boundaries, she would not be in my life.

"But she did. So she is."

Alex: "This sounds great in theory, but...my mom hurt me so much. I just figured this out. How can I forgive her? I'm still angry!"

Dr. Kate: "You don't have to forgive her now. In fact, you should *not* forgive her if you're still angry. That would be what's called a bypass."

Alex: "Oh yeah, Dr. Dan talked about that. He called it 'spiritual bypass.' He said I need to feel my anger first, and once I do that and let it go, then I can start forgiving."

Dr. Kate: "He's right. Take the time you need to feel your emotions. In fact, I would not recommend reaching out until you're ready to forgive her. That might take time."

Alex: "I feel like I just realized how mad at her I was and now I have to forgive her."

Dr. Kate: "You don't have to do anything. This is a choice. But Alex, being human means making mistakes. When we're able to acknowledge this fact, we can forgive ourselves, and we can begin correcting our mistakes—which you have, to your credit.

"And once we forgive ourselves, we can forgive anyone. Including our parents."

I thought about this. What a lot to digest. This is like riding a roller coaster. I keep getting whipped around in all directions, and just when I think it's done, I get surprised by something I didn't see coming at all. I felt like I was never stable or comfortable.

Then, I realized that's how roller coasters are designed. They're supposed to surprise you with twists and turns. That's the point.

Alex: "Okay, I'll reach out. But, seriously, what do I say? How do I frame the conversation? I can't begin by telling her she was a bad mom, can I?"

Dr. Kate: "That would not be helpful, no. Why not start with your wants and needs? Do you want a relationship with her? And if so, what do you need from her to make that happen? Then, perhaps, listen to her needs, if she's able to express them."

I paused and thought about it.

Alex: "Honestly…I want her to be the mom she never was."

The look she gave me…love mixed with heartbreak? I don't know. It was sad though.

Dr. Kate: "I'm not sure that can happen, Alex. The time for her to be the mom you needed when you were a child is past and cannot return. But the two of you can create something new, together. And if not, you can move forward and have the life you want, without her."

Alex: "So, I can't ask her to be my mom?"

Dr. Kate: "Again, you can do anything you want. But that's close to a demand. Making demands isn't the best way to build a relationship. That is, in essence, what your mom did to you, though probably very unconsciously."

Alex: "How do I build a relationship then?"

Dr. Kate: *"You can tell her your needs and your boundaries. She can tell you hers, and then the two of you can negotiate how to engage and both meet each other's needs, if that's possible. That's how healthy relationships are built."*

Alex: "What if I don't know what my needs are? I'm not even sure how to set boundaries with my mom."

Dr. Kate: "That's why you're here. That's what we'll figure out together."

Alex: "Why haven't I thought about my dad in any of these sessions, except just a few times in passing? He wasn't perfect either. If anything, I felt like he'd be more of the issue. He left us when I was young."

Dr. Kate: "I'd guess it's not time to heal that wound. Start where you are, and then let everything else come as it comes."

CHAPTER 28

The Preparation

It was about a month later when I decided I was ready to call my mom.

Dr. Kate helped me work through a lot of my anger. Not all of it, of course. But a lot. I felt I wouldn't lash out at my mom, and that I'd processed and let go of enough to be ready.

We'd really worked on figuring out what my needs and boundaries were. I was kind of shocked to realize how bad my boundaries were and how much shit I put up with in my life. I never thought of myself as a pushover, but I was. And for no other reason than I let people do it to me.

At a Sunday dinner, I told Pa Bill and Granny Jane about my plan to call my mom. I thought they'd be excited, but they weren't. Granny Jane didn't seem to want to talk about it, and Pa moved on to another subject.

Then, after dinner, Pa took me out to his office in the barn to talk.

Pa: "Son, I know you're going to call you mom, and that's great.

I hope it goes well. I just want you to know something I learned the hard way in Vietnam:

"Everyone believes they're the good guy."

Alex: "What do you mean?"

Pa: "Everyone believes they're right, that what they're doing is the right thing to do. And they tell themselves whatever story they need to tell to make that feel true to them."

Alex: "How'd you learn this in Vietnam?"

Pa gave me that look he gives when I ask a stupid question. I always laugh at him because it's so funny, and he always laughs back.

Then, a weird thought flashed into my head.

He'd always delivered that look to me with love. What I'd never thought about, though, was what that look must have been like delivered in a stern angry way.

He could melt ice when he looked at you angrily. I'd seen that a few times, and it struck real fear into me. Which is probably what my mom had gotten from him as a kid. I'd never really thought about that before.

Pa: "I told you I was in military intelligence in 'Nam, right? I spent most of my time in an office without air conditioning, going over reports, and making plans and all of that bureaucratic BS you have to do. But every now and then, I'd go with the real snake eaters out into the field, and I'd talk to captured Viet Cong.

"Once I started interrogating those VC, I realized something that shocked me:

"They thought they were the good guys!

"That whole idea blew me away. How the HELL could these fellas think *they* are the good guys? We were *obviously* the good guys. And none of 'em could give me a good answer until I met Dien Hwook Min.

"He was a high-level officer in the VC, and we'd captured him. The real high speed interrogators wouldn't get there for two days, so I was tasked with softening him up and seeing what I could get. I was the good cop."

Alex: "You're a big guy, Pa. Why didn't you play 'bad cop' and beat his ass?"

Pa: "That's movie bullshit. You don't get info from people by beatin 'em. That just stiffens their resolve. I figured that out quick, and I was just a country boy then.

"Anyway, I spent two days talking to him. He was real smart. This guy spoke five languages, went to university in France, and by then, he'd been leading VC units for years against some of America's best boys—and whoopin 'em.

"Here I was, barely graduated high school and only in military intelligence because I got a near perfect score on the IQ test they give to recruits—which your Granny is still tickled by all these years later. I tell her I cheated on it."

Alex: "Granny tells that story all the time, that she knew you were smart, and that she didn't need a government test to tell her that."

Pa: "Anyway, I was young, shiny, and spit-polished. I'd bought 100 percent of our story—hook, line, and sinker. We were the good guys, there to help the poor farmers fight off the Communists. They were slaughtering babies in the street, and we were gonna save 'em.

"But this was the first person I'd ever met in my life that saw it a different way and could explain it to me. I didn't admit it at the time, not to my buddies or superiors or even to myself—but that guy got in my head."

Alex: "Really? YOU?!"

Pa: "Oh yeah. Yer making the same mistake the asshole politicians made—underestimatin' 'em."

Alex: "I'm just surprised. How'd he do it?"

Pa: "Remember, I was much younger then. I was pretty idealistic. And foolish, to be honest. I didn't know anything about the way the world really worked. What he did to twist me up was real simple: he explained *why* his side were the good guys.

"He told me how he'd studied the American founding fathers and our history. He knew his stuff, better than me. He quoted the damn Declaration of Independence to me. Taught me stuff I didn't know, like Jefferson had kids with his slaves. I had no idea about that then.

"Anyway, he told me a story about how he decided he would

join the VC. He told me about how the South Vietnamese government killed his family, and that he felt a deep bond with America's founding fathers and their struggle, and he saw the current day America the way the founding fathers saw the British empire. As an occupying force invading and trying to take his freedom.

"I tried to argue with him, but how do you do that? How do you tell a man who wanted to be free to live peacefully on his own land that we are the good guys when, in fact, the government we were supporting killed his family and took his land?

"I'll be damned if I didn't see his point of view. It changed me."

Then, Pa got emotional. In a way I'd never seen. He didn't cry, but I could tell this hit him deep. He paused, and he looked away for what seemed like an hour.

Pa: "When he explained that…nothing was the same after that. At least nothing about the war."

Alex: "What'd you do?"

Pa: "You know I enlisted voluntarily, right? This was back when there was a draft, and people were burning their draft cards and moving to Canada. I walked into the recruiting office and signed up.

"After I got myself cleaned up, I'd planned to make the military my career. Your granny and I talked about it, and she agreed. It was the best path out for guys like me, who came from nothing.

"But that one conversation…I couldn't do it after that.

"I still love America, but I love America in the way the original founders did. I don't think we need to be in other people's business. Don't get me wrong; I didn't turn into no dope-smoking hippy. But still, I couldn't find a good answer to why we were in Vietnam. So, I left the military when my tour was up. Then I worked construction, then started my own business, and here we are."

Alex: "Wow. I didn't know this at all."

Pa: "I've told you my good war stories. That one's harder to tell. Anyway, the reason I'm telling you is because it applies to your mom. She thinks I was the bad guy, and she's the good guy. And maybe, in some ways, that's true. In fact, in some ways, I know it's true. I wasn't the father to her that she needed all the time."

Alex: "In what way?"

Pa paused and looked away again.

Pa: "I was just very hard on her and yelled a lot and was just...strict. I thought I was a great dad 'cause I never hit her, but well...I've come to realize that's not a high standard for fatherhood."

Alex: "You did the best you could at the time, didn't you?"

Pa: "Yeah, of course, I did. I thought I was doing right. But I wasn't. And that's hard to deal with. I'm in my late seventies, and I'm still learning what Dien Hwook Min taught me. Everyone has their own perspective. For years, I only saw things from my perspective with your mom."

Alex: "Yeah, Dr. Kate talks about this a lot. She says the way we're treated as small children is the way we treat ourselves the rest of our lives. If we were treated with cruelty, that's how we treat our kids. And that most parents just put all the bullshit they suffered onto their kids. Even if we do better with our kids than our parents did to us, we still do it. Unless we do our healing first."

Pa: "Yeah, I can see that. I always told myself I was a better parent to her than I got, and I was, but that's not a high standard for parenting either."

Alex: "You know Pa, it's not too late to make this right."

Pa looked away again, and when he did, I realized I was crying a little.

Pa "I'm telling you this…I'm thinking when you reach out to her, she'll do the same to you. I know she will because she did this to you as a kid. She still does it. She only sees things from her perspective, and she'll make herself the good guy and everyone else the bad guy. It's how she does it.

"But, son: give her some space to let that stuff out. I'm not saying to take shit from her or let her hurt you or anything like that. But I know she's real hurt, and I don't think she's done anything to deal with that, and a lot of that is my fault. And it tears me up inside."

Alex: "Yeah, okay."

I thought about his statement for a second, and then I thought about what Dr. Kate always says to me.

Alex: "Pa, you know, you aren't responsible for her emotions. I mean, yeah, you may not have been the best dad, and yeah, you should probably apologize for that...but you can't blame yourself for how she feels now. Her emotions are ultimately her responsibility."

Pa gave me a look I've never seen from him before. It was quizzical, but also...impressed? It's not like him to be impressed by anything, but I swear that was his facial expression.

Pa: "From the mouths of fucking babes over here. That damn MDMA has really worked on you, son!"

Alex: "That's what Dr. Kate says to me all the time, at least. I think she's right."

He looked at me again, then away for a long time. Then came back with tears in his eyes and put his huge hand on my arm.

Pa: "You're right; I should apologize to her. I never have, and she deserves it. I've tried, but you know how she is—I can't get an apology out before she is sniping at me and all that. Then I get angry, and we start fighting, and you know how it goes with her.

"I guess that's my excuse, though.

"But what I'm trying to say is...you may be her son, but right now, you could be more mature than her in some ways. One day I'll tell you how I had to be a parent to my parents, but trust me when I tell you—it's a very rough feeling. I just wanted you to know it might be coming for you."

Alex: "Oh. I hadn't thought about it that way at all."

Pa: "Yeah. It's not fun when it happens. But I think you can handle it, if you have to."

The next week, Anne and I got lunch together.

Alex: "Oh, I forgot to tell you this: I got this message super clear in my last session. I have no idea what it means, but I'm supposed to ask you about your boyfriend?"

She gave me a weird look.

Anne: "We broke up last week."

Alex: "On no! I liked Oliver a lot."

Anne: "Yeah, I did too. He's a good guy."

Alex: "You were engaged. I'd never even known you when you weren't dating him."

Anne: "You're not making this easier."

We laughed at my callousness. I didn't mean it that way at all, but yeah, she was totally right.

Alex: "I'm really sorry. What happened?"

Anne: "We just…grew apart. You'll see this happen to you as well—as you go on this journey, not everyone in your life will come with you. It's sad, but it happens."

Alex: "Yeah, Dr. Dan talked about this."

Anne: "He's right. The same thing happened with my dad."

Alex: "What do you mean? What happened?"

Anne: "Well, as I got better, he got angrier."

Alex: "How?"

Anne: "When I told him about my needs, he'd make snide comments. Or when I would hold a boundary, he'd get upset and tell me I made him feel bad. Lots and lots of things like that. It eventually got to the point where I didn't want to be around that behavior."

Alex: "I'm sorry. You didn't tell me about this."

Anne: "It's very recent."

We sat next to each other, just being together, for a few minutes. I didn't know what to say.

Anne had been very close to her dad, and I remember in the beginning him being happy for her that she was doing this therapy. And we had talked about how excited she was to connect deeper with her parents and mend that relationship.

Anne: "This is a harsh truth I learned, and my therapist warned me: your healing could bring out the emotional immaturity of your parents. It was great with my mom; she responded really well. And my dad too. But then, he turned. It started a while ago, and it kept building.

"The weird thing is I feel like the same thing happened with

Oliver. I never saw the similarities between them, but now, it's kind of shocking. They both encouraged me to do this, and then both got upset as I grew from it."

Alex: "I'm sorry."

Anne: "Yeah. I've been doing my work for a year, and things were hard at first, then got amazing, and now they're hard again."

Alex: "I guess this is how healing works, isn't it? Weren't you the one who told me that?"

Anne: "That's what I'm learning again, yeah."

As I got closer to reaching out to my mom, Dr. Kate helped me understand that there are four steps to effective communication:

First, you observe a situation.

Then, you recognize the feelings that this situation brings up in you.

Then, you examine what needs of yours are related to these feelings.

Finally, you look at what you can ask for in concrete terms to satisfy these needs.

I was lost at first, but then she asked for an example of how my mom might communicate with me in a way that I disliked. So, I gave her an example of the type of thing my mother would say to me when I lived with her in high school:

"Why is your room always messy? I tell you to clean it up, and you never do because you're a lazy good-for-nothing! You never do anything right! How hard is it to just pick up after yourself?!"

But she reframed it and showed me how she would express the same idea to her son:

"When I see your things lying around the living room [*observation*], this puts me in a bad mood [*feeling*] because I need the spaces that we share to be tidier [*need*]. Could you put them away? [*request*]."

That was a world of difference.

She called this "non-violent communication," and it seemed super touchy-feely to me at first, but we practiced it for a long time, and once I got used to it, I really liked it.

It was all about taking full responsibility for my emotions and talking in terms of my needs but without judging the other person. It made total sense.

We practiced for many sessions until I felt like I got it. After the medicine work, the integration, the talks with my pa and granny, and everything else, I was ready to talk to my mom again.

CHAPTER 29

The Call

I put the day and time I was going to call on my calendar a week before. And as the time came, I sat there staring at the phone, honestly not sure what would happen when I called.

I had no idea how my mom would react. Or how I would react.

I wasn't even entirely sure what this call would do.

I tried to not attach to any outcome. If we mended our relationship, great. If not, I could live with that too. I just knew that my relationship with my mom was a deep and unhealed wound, and that reaching out was the first step to healing.

I looked at Murph, curled up at my side on the sofa.

Alex: "Whatcha think, girl? Ready to help me call Mom?"

She wagged her tail and licked my hand. My palms were sweating as I dialed the number, and after the third ring, I assumed my mom wouldn't pick up, so I got ready to leave a message. Then, an out of breath voice came on.

Mom: "Alex?! Is everything okay?!"

Alex: "Hi, Mom…uhhh, yeah, of course. Why?"

Mom: "You're calling me out of the blue; I assume someone died."

I could feel the emotions start to well up. She hadn't even said, "Hi," and she was criticizing me already? *What the fuck. This was a mistake, and I should hang up.*

No…calm down. Give her a chance. I did call her out of the blue after all.

Alex: "No, Mom. Everything is fine."

Mom: "Oh. Okay."

Alex: "How are you?"

Mom: "Fine. I haven't heard from you in a while."

This is why I never called her. Everything she says is a criticism.

I sighed and took a deep breath. I honestly didn't even think she understood that she does this.

Alex: "Well, I'm calling now. I would like to talk. Would you?"

Mom: "Yeah. I mean…if you want to."

God, she's like a child. This is awful.

Then, I chuckled to myself. Now I can see what Dr. Kate means.

Yes, she's doing all the things I am complaining about, but still, this is her stuff. *I am complaining about her instead of focusing on me and my needs.*

I took a deep breath and recentered.

Alex: "How have you been?"

Mom: "Lonely. I mean, you never call."

What the fuck!

Stop. Deep breath. Time to use what Dr. Kate and I practiced.

Alex: "Mom, when you say things like that, I feel bad because I experience it as you criticizing me. Could you please not do that?"

Mom: "Say things like what?"

Alex: "You told me I never call."

Mom: "You don't."

Alex: "Well, I am calling now, aren't I?"

Mom: "Why didn't you call before?"

I was about to say, "Why didn't you call me?" but then we'd be in a fight, and it would spiral.

And all at once, the memories and images from the medicine and therapy sessions came together and everything made sense. It was like all the puzzle pieces clicked together in my head.

She would attack me for not meeting her needs.

I would react defensively and attack her back.

She would use my reaction as proof of her rightness and counterattack. Rinse and repeat, forever.

My god…this cycle had been going for our whole lives.

I wasn't going to do it anymore. I was going to break this cycle with truth, compassion, self-respect, and boundaries.

Alex: "I didn't call because I didn't enjoy talking to you. I felt sad when I talked to you in the past."

Mom: "What? What kind of son says that to his mother?"

Alex: "The kind who is honest about his emotions and needs."

Mom: "Well, what about my needs?"

Alex "Would you like to discuss them?"

She was so stunned, she couldn't respond for a second.

Alex: "I'm telling you what I need from our conversation. That's all. You are welcome to do the same."

Mom: "I need you to not disrespect me."

Alex: "How did I disrespect you?"

Mom: "You said I made you feel bad!"

Alex: "No, I did not. I am responsible for my own emotions, and I would never blame you for how I feel. I simply told you how I felt when you made certain types of comments and asked you not to make them."

I felt like Neo in *The Matrix*, when he dodges bullets for the first time. I could see this whole thing playing out in slow motion in front of me.

Mom: "Well...I..."

Alex: "I would like to discuss if we can possibly have a relationship and what that would entail. Would you be willing to do that?"

Mom: "Yes."

The rest of the conversation went the same as the first part, with one major shift:

Because I stopped reacting to my mom's attacks and simply held my boundaries, stated my needs, and then listened to hers, by the end of the call, she calmed down. We finished the call by planning to talk again soon.

I got off the call and noticed I was sweating. But I also felt elated. I felt like I had dumped a thousand pounds off my back.

No, my relationship with my mom was not healed. No, my mom was not much different than she had been my whole life.

But I was different. I had changed.

The medicine had worked, my work had paid off, and I was a different person. I was on the path to be who I wanted to be, regardless of what my mom did or did not do.

And I'd only just started.

CHAPTER 30

Integration Session: "How do I know when I'm done?"

Dr. Dan: "Alex, you look fantastic. How are you feeling?"

Alex: "I feel really good. I honestly can't say enough about how great everything has been. I mean, don't get me wrong: it's been hard, but it's also been the best thing I've ever done."

Dr. Dan: "I'm so glad to hear that. Do you want to catch me up to how things went for you?"

I filled Dr. Dan in on everything: the call with my mom, the story Pa told me, what Dr. Kate and Anne helped me with—everything.

Dr. Dan: "Let me just, again, reflect your hard work back to you and celebrate all the progress that you've made. It's tremendous to see your change from before medicine work to now. To get to the place that you're in and to begin to find compassion, forgiveness, and self-acceptance—this is just fantastic."

Alex: "Thanks, Dr. Dan."

Dr. Dan: "The willingness to do this work and engage your mother and grandparents in this conversation, to heal yourself so that you're not passing on the transgenerational trauma that was passed onto you, that's really incredible."

Alex: "Thanks, I wasn't so sure about all of this at first, but I'm so glad I did it and so glad I listened to your advice."

Dr. Dan smiled. He seemed genuinely happy. Not in a 'I feel good because someone complimented me' way either. He seemed legitimately happy for me. It's a strange feeling, when someone is happy for you just for you, and I wasn't not sure I'd ever seen it before this radiantly, but it was there.

Alex: "Can I ask you some more questions before we go?"

Dr. Dan: "Of course."

Alex: "It seems like I feel my emotions way more. And even deeper than that. I feel so sensitive to everything now. And I don't necessarily mean it in a bad way, like I get offended or anything. I mean I just *feel* things more. Is that normal?"

Dr. Dan: "That's totally normal."

Alex: "What does that mean?"

Dr. Dan: "Have you ever broken a bone and had to wear a cast?"

Alex: "Yeah, my arm."

Dr. Dan: "How'd your arm feel once you got the cast off?"

Alex: "Really sensitive."

Dr. Dan: "Exactly. You touch it and it's like, 'Whoa.' Everything is starting to wake up. Eventually, it becomes sensitized into the next phase of its healing and function. But when you take the cast off, it's super sensitive.

"That's an analogy I like to use for medicine work. We experience trauma, and then build up a 'cast' to protect ourselves. Except the cast doesn't come off. And we become numb and desensitized to most stuff.

"This medicine comes, cuts the cast off, and now our psyches are quite sensitive."

Alex: "Yeah, that makes sense."

Dr. Dan: "It's not just feeling love; you feel everything. When the heart starts to open, it's not only selective for the good stuff. It means also being willing to feel what may be uncomfortable, like the projection from other people."

Alex: "I think I understand that, but can you give me an example?"

Dr. Dan: "I'll use an example from my own life. Just today I got cursed out by a little old lady! I was pulling out of a parking spot, and I guess I was in her way. She laid on the horn for a long time. I said to myself, 'Is someone honking at me. Me?'

"I turned around to look, and she leaned out her window, flashed a double middle finger to me, and screamed at the top of her lungs, 'FUUUUUUCK YOOOOOOU!'"

I just burst out laughing.

Alex: "I'm sorry, Dr. Dan; I'm not laughing at you; I'm just imagining my granny doing that, and it's an amazing mental picture."

Dr. Dan: "Oh, it was. Honestly, it freaked me out. I was like, 'Holy cow, I just got double imprinted by an eighty-year-old lady.'

"Then, I felt super sad. I'm like, 'Wow, she's walking around in her everyday life like that.'

"Then, I was freaked out even more because I thought, 'Wow, is this the state of humanity?'

"I realized that for many people, yes, it was. And I got sad again because I realized, 'Holy shit, we've got a lot of work to do.' It stuck me into this little spiral for a while.

"But then I thought, 'Could I have just like been a little nicer and not so freaked out? Maybe like if I knew where she lived, I could just go give her a random flower on her doorstep, maybe that would've made her day?'"

I started laughing again.

Alex: "I'm sorry, Dr. Dan; I don't mean to laugh, but I had no idea you were such a softie. Man, when I said sensitive, I didn't mean giving flowers to people who flip me off! I'm not criticizing you, but I'm not close to this. I'm just, like, feeling my emotions for the first time."

Dr. Dan: "Let me be clear: I did not start here. Like I told you before, I'm way more sensitive than I used to be."

Alex: "That actually brings up a good question: what's next for me and the medicine? Is there another program to go through like the last one?"

Dr. Dan: "Yes and no. I'd say you've gone through a really strong arc of experience over these last three sessions. Give it at least six months to integrate, and let's see where you are then.

"Six months is a good amount of time for most people to put into action all the lessons they've learned through an arc of medicine work, and it helps them level up to live their lives based on the day-to-day practice of those lessons.

"So, yes, there could be more if you want to pursue it, and yes, I'd be happy to help you understand what's next."

Alex: "Do I take different medicines then?"

Dr. Dan: "Possibly. After six months of integration, if you're curious to investigate or try another tool like psilocybin or aya-huasca, that might make sense. It really depends on where you are, how you're feeling, and what you're looking for."

Alex: "I guess this brings up the question: do I ever get fully healed? Or am I just on a journey forever now?"

Dr. Dan: "I like Joseph Campbell's quote. 'A well-lived life is one hero's journey after another.'

"I do believe that we are becoming whole and fully switched on to the awesomeness of who we are and who everybody is—that's a process, and it runs in cycles that never really end."

Alex: "So, I just keep doing the same integration practice?"

Dr. Dan: "Yep, exactly the same."

Alex: "Why isn't there a checklist for integration? There's a checklist for a medicine session."

Dr. Dan: "Because there are so many potential ways to integrate. And beyond that, a checklist would miss the point. In some ways, the struggle of finding the right integration practice is part of the work. It forces you to get to know yourself. Everyone's journey is different, but even if I knew yours, I wouldn't tell you. Figuring it out is the point."

Alex: "I've found myself talking to my friends about this a lot. I want to tell people to do this work, but what's the best way to do that if they're interested?"

Dr. Dan: "Yeah, it's super enticing to be an evangelist for this kind of work. But let me be very clear about this:

"The best way to share this work is to do your work first, so your life is an example of your work.

"This is essentially what Gandhi was saying about becoming the change you wish to see in the world. Even more specifically, it's related to one of my favorite teachers, St. Francis of Assisi, when he said 'share the gospel with everyone, and when necessary use words.'

"This makes even more sense when we remember that gospel means good news. And this is exactly what you're starting to do: share the good news. This type of mindful medicine work is available, and it does work. So, talking about it is fine—but only as an extension of living it and being it."

Alex: "Oh man, you sound like my pa. He's always telling me to let my actions speak louder than my words and to be the example of what I say."

Dr. Dan: "He's right. When you do that, those that are closest to you are going to see it, and they're going to get super curious."

Alex: "Okay, I can do that."

Dr. Dan: "Another important thing is the way you share it. I like to use 'I' statements about how it benefited me verses talking about how it will benefit another. Basically, I just talk about my own process. I say things like,

"'I learned more about myself.'

"'I learned about how to love, how to forgive.'

"'I learned about all this stuff I was holding in the background that I didn't even remember.'

"Begin with 'I' statements first. If people are curious about how that happened, then you might describe the process that you went through.

"Lastly, a very helpful thing to do is to give people information. Point people in the right direction to where they can get really good, clear information: websites to go to, documentaries to see, books to read, etc. You still have the resource sheet I gave you?"

Alex: "Yeah."

Dr. Dan: "Feel free to give that to anyone or direct them to the copy that's online."

Alex: "I think I have a good handle on that because of how Anne did it with me. She never told me what to do; she just modeled the change, and then I was curious and pestered her. Then, she told me where to go, but she didn't do it for me.

"Another question: I know I'm not ready now, but what about working in this field and helping people do their work. Is that even possible? And if it is, what do I do?"

Dr. Dan: "It's very natural to want to see what you've experienced happen for others and to potentially be a part of their process too. There's a variety of different ways that people support others through this work.

"Sometimes it's just giving them information on where they can go to get this work done.

"But if you mean to actually facilitate this work, as I do, it's pretty necessary to have mentorship, guidance, and to actually go through a thorough curriculum and a training program in order to do that. I wouldn't do this casually with friends."

Alex: "I'm not going to, but I'm just curious. Why not?"

Dr. Dan: "Licensed facilitators engaged in this work have training and background in psychotherapy or counseling or coaching. And they're trained in understanding the nuances of altered states of consciousness and transpersonal states and how to weave in trauma recovery work and shadow work into an organized system of therapeutic healing.

One of the challenges of this work can be when trauma spontaneously comes up and the facilitator doesn't know how to work with it. It can become really uncomfortable for everybody involved if the trauma gets revealed but not worked through.

"There are a lot of other things to take into consideration, but this is one of the biggest."

Alex: "One last question, Dr. Dan. This might be a heavy one. I don't know how to say this, but I feel like I may have talked to…I don't want to say 'God,' but I felt a God-like energy during my last session. What's going on there? Am I going crazy?"

Dr. Dan: "Absolutely not. This is very normal and natural and ties back into your question about feeling more.

"The relationship we have to—let's call it—'Source' is very personal. It doesn't have to look like anybody else's.

"It happens to be that we live in a culture right now that tends to compartmentalize spirituality into religious context. And when religion gets so constrained and contracted into believing it's the only way, it becomes a dogma and then starts to persecute and project wrongness or invalidation of other spiritual practices and experiences.

"So, my invitation to you would be to follow what feels authentically right for you, spiritually.

"To want to investigate our own consciousness—in states of silence and inner vision and introspection, through meditation and flotation and writing and walking in nature—can be one of the most spiritual practices to have.

"Everybody's path to spirituality is going to look unique, and my invitation would be to continue to follow that thing that lights you up the most. That gets you the most connected to continuously growing, excited states of love and joy and unity the most.

"I absolutely believe that everything is a part of the same Source. We're all made from the same cosmic dust. Everything is born of the same cycles. Just as the seasons have their cycles, and the animals and the plants and the cosmic bodies have their cycles. Just like stars go through birth and death, and cells go through birth and death, and everything else on the planet goes through birth and death. So, will we."

I stopped and thought about what he said.

Alex: "Thanks, Dr. Dan. This has been great."

Dr. Dan: "I'm so happy for you, Alex; you've really done great. You have many new opportunities in front of you. I'm really excited to see the ones that you decide to take and where you take them."

Alex: "I'm really excited to talk to you in six months about going deeper as well."

Dr. Dan: "I look forward to it."

CHAPTER 31

The Return

I filled Dr. Kate in on the conversation.

Dr Kate: "I'm so happy for you, Alex."

This was the happiest I'd ever seen her. I realized something really hard: I'd never seen that look from my mom before.

I wanted to cry.

Alex: "Thank you, Dr. Kate. I couldn't have done this without you."

Dr. Kate: "It's my pleasure. You are the reason I do this. To help you—and people just like you—do exactly what you're doing. I get the greatest joy from it."

Alex: "I felt so down a few months ago, and now I kind of feel on top of the world right now. Like anything is possible."

Dr. Kate: "For you, Alex, it is. I truly believe that."

Alex: "So, what's next in the process?"

Dr. Kate: "That's up to you. Healing runs in cycles, and you just completed a cycle. Right now is the optimal time to rest and integrate everything that has happened. Your next cycle will emerge soon enough. But let's make sure to celebrate how far you've come and what you've accomplished."

Alex: "In some ways, I feel like I've won, but in other ways, I feel like…the real game actually just began."

Dr. Kate: "That's very wise. You're right on both accounts."

✶ ✶ ✶

I could hardly wait to tell my grandparents about the conversation with my mom.

Pa: "Son, that went about as good as I could have imagined. I'm so proud of you."

Granny: "I'm just happy that everyone is getting along again."

Alex: "Yeah, Pa, I know what you mean now about taking care of your parents. It was weird. I got the distinct feeling that I was parenting her in a way."

Granny gave Pa a look. I couldn't quite tell what she meant. I swear those two could read each other's minds, which I guess happens when you've been together for fifty years.

Pa: "No, I didn't tell him."

Alex: "Tell me what?"

She looked at him again.

Pa: "About my parents."

Alex: "You mean what you said at the last dinner? About parenting them?"

Pa: "We'll talk about that later. What I want to talk about now is when my session is going to be."

Alex: "Your session for what?"

Pa: "Son, are you dense? My MDMA session! What else would I be talking about, my tar and feathering session?"

Alex: "What? For real?"

Pa: "Have you ever known me to be a joker? Of course, I'm for real! I already told you I might do it after you did. And seeing you make all these amazing changes, I can't just sit here with my thumb up my ass, can I? I'm proud as hell of you, but you ain't the only one in the family who has the courage to change."

Alex: "I...I had no idea you were still considering it. You didn't mention it again after that first time."

Pa: "I was waiting for you to be done. I didn't want to step into that. But now that you're done, you think you can introduce me to that guide of yours? What's his name, Dr. Dan? You think he'd do well for me?"

I thought about it for a second, and out of nowhere, the ballsiest idea came into my head.

Alex: "I can do you one better. I will introduce you to someone on his team, Dr. Naomi. She's much more your speed. I think you'd really like her and connect well with her. *But*—I will only do it under two conditions."

He gave me his 'negotiation eyes.' I've seen him stare down the snakiest real estate developers with these eyes.

Pa: "Go on."

Alex: "First, I want you to teach me how to start and run my own business. I'm tired of my job, and I want to do something else. I don't know what, but I can figure that out later.

"Second, I want you to talk to Dr. Kate and at least consider seeing her as a therapist. The medicine alone isn't enough, even with Dr. Naomi. You need a therapist too. And she would be perfect for you."

He gave me a look I'd never seen before. It was part awe, part amusement, part…amusement?

And then he burst out laughing.

Pa: "You little son of a gun! I'll be!

"The business thing: I would *love* to do that! I've been waiting for you to ask me about that for years. I hate that stupid company you work for, and I would be damn excited to help you start any sort of business you want.

"As for therapy, hells bells, son—after Dr. Kate taught you how to handle your mother, I believe she could teach a lion to hunt. Sign me up for that woman right now."

Further Reading

Dr. Dan gave Alex this list of material to research on trauma, therapy, psychedelics, and the path of getting to know oneself.

Regarding the inheritance of transgenerational trauma patterns:

It Didn't Start with You
By Mark Wolynn

Regarding the broader field of psychedelic therapy and its twentieth-century history:

How to Change Your Mind
By Michael Pollan

Regarding the importance of listening to one's inner guide and the benefit of taking a journey outside of the known in order to find the treasure inside:

The Alchemist
By Paulo Coelho

Dr. Kate recommended this book to Alex to help him understand the dynamics of parental emotional abuse and neglect:

The Drama of the Gifted Child
by Alice Miller

There are many other books by Alice Miller and books about this subject, if you want to dive deeper, but start with this book, as it is the foundation of her work.

Discussing trauma, Dr. Kate focused on the research of Peter Levine and Bessel Van Der Kirk. If you want to learn about trauma and how it affects people, these books are a great place to start:

The Body Keeps the Score: Brain, Mind, and Body in the Healing of Trauma
By Bessel Van Der Kirk

In an Unspoken Voice: How the Body Releases Trauma and Restores Goodness
By Peter A. Levine

When helping Alex learn how to talk to his mother, Dr. Kate used many of the principles outlined in this book:

Non-Violent Communication: A Language of Life
By Marshall Rosenberg

References and Sources on MDMA

Feduccia, Allison A., Lisa Jerome, Berra Yazar-Klosinski, Amy Emerson, Michael C Mithoefer, and Rick Doblin. "Breakthrough for Trauma Treatment: Safety and Efficacy of MDMA-Assisted Psychotherapy Compared to Paroxetine and Sertraline." *Frontiers in Psychiatry* (September 12, 2019). https://doi.org/10.3389/fpsyt.2019.00650.

Grinage, Bradley D. "Diagnosis and Management of Post-Traumatic Stress Disorder." *American Family Physician* 68, no. 12 (December 15, 2003). https://www.aafp.org/afp/2003/1215/p2401.html.

Jerome, Lisa, Allison A. Feduccia, Julie B. Wang, et al. "Long-Term Follow-Up Outcomes of MDMA-Assisted Psychotherapy for Treatment of PTSD: A Longitudinal Pooled Analysis of Six Phase 2 Trials." *Psychopharmacology* 237 (August 2020). https://doi.org/10.1007/s00213-020-05548-2.

Ot'alora G., Marcela, Jim Grigsby, Bruce Poulter, Joseph W. Van Derveer, Sara Gael Giron, Lisa Jerome, Allison A. Feduccia, Scott Hamilton, Berra Yazar-Klosinski, Amy Emerson, Michael C. Mithoefer, Rick Dobli. "3,4-Methylenedioxymethamphetamine-assisted psychotherapy for treatment of chronic posttraumatic stress disorder: A randomized phase 2 controlled trial." *Journal of Psychopharmacology* 32, no. 12 (October 29, 2018). https://doi.org/10.1177/0269881118806297

Metcalf, Olivia, Caleb Stone, Mark Hinton, Meaghan O'Donnell, Malcolm Hopwood, Alexander McFarlane, David Forbes, et al. "Treatment augmentation for posttraumatic stress disorder: A systematic review." *Clinical Psychology: Science and Practice* 27, no. 1 (December 22, 2019). https://doi.org/10.1111/cpsp.12310.

Watkins, Laura E., Kelsey R. Sprang, and Barbara O. Rothbaum. "Treating PTSD: A Review of Evidence-Based Psychotherapy Interventions." *Frontiers in Behavioral Neuroscience* (November 2, 2018). https://doi.org/10.3389/fnbeh.2018.00258.

Acknowledgments

DR. DAN ENGLE

Thanks are not enough to express my gratitude to the many teachers who have taken the time to guide me along the path of Transformational Medicine.

With one hand over my heart and the other raised high, special shout outs of thanks go to:

The pioneers in the arena of Psychedelic Therapy: Jim Fadiman, Stan Grof, Gabor Mate, Francoise Bourzat, Kate Hawke, Rick Doblin, Will Van Derveer, to name only a few I've been graced to know. We each stand on the shoulders of the giants who have come before.

The organizations promoting this work in a good way: MAPS, Horizons, The Beckley Foundation, ICEERS, Johns Hopkins, Psychedelic Times, Being True to You and Reset.me. There are more curious travelers rising every day, and each of you is helping guide the way.

The voices: My brothers, Aubrey Marcus and Porangui Carvalho McGrew; two new epic friends in the field, Tim Ferriss and Ben Greenfield; my sisters Samantha Sweetwater and Puma St Angel; the living libraries of Graham Hancock and Wade Davis; and the heavy weight of psychedelic storylines, Joe Rogan. Story moves culture. Bring it!

My teachers of the Shamanic Path: Don Howard Lawler, Javier Regueiro, Percy Garcia, Andre, and all our plant allies. In continued awe of the majesty of your work, I salute you.

My teachers of Various Spiritual Traditions: Paramahansa Yogananda, Thubten Chodron, Jiddu Krishnamurti, Sri Aurobindo, Mary Magdalen, Master Jesus and Saint Germain. Countless beings have received the benefit of your legendary consciousness teachings. We all salute you.

My teachers in the West: Roger Bell, Hyla Cass, Emilio Romero, Gabriel Cousins, and Rob Cass. You've each been a mentor of epic proportions.

My co-author: There is indeed life before medicine work and life after medicine work, and it's been a privilege to support your process.

My partner, Sonya Anita: The most amazing woman I've ever known. Without your radical love and feminine genius, this book would have taken many more years to emerge from the assorted backpacks and journals, and I would have taken many decades more to find freedom through commitment.

The litany of my beautiful friends and allies: My incredible blood family and my Sedona soul tribe, your unwavering support was a beacon in the darkness, my co-founder Guenter Bergman in our Kuya Clinic, we're just getting started. The one hundred, plus, additional fabulous holders of my heart not named here and all of my yet-to-have-met family along this Path of Awakening. The psychedelic renaissance is upon us.

With reverence, fellowship, and celebration, may we each do what is ours to do.

ALEX YOUNG

I can't thank too many people, given the pen name and all.

Of course, my husband, children, and animals are always first.

I must thank Dr. Dan, who's been my guide through so much growth and change. If it weren't for him and his extended family of kind and skilled healers, I shudder to think where I might be. I owe them so very much. Writing this book was not just a joy and privilege, but the very least I could do to give back. I hope it can make a small contribution to this important movement and to the healing of others.

I must thank my therapist. You know who you are and what you've meant to me. Dr. Kate is based largely on you.

I also want to thank the whole Scribe Media team, who were absolutely wonderful to work with. I'm so happy that a company exists like yours that both provides a professional publishing model for authors, as well as openly discusses and promotes this type of spiritual work with its people.

And a special thanks to Tucker, Oliver, Emily, Sherry, Nate,

Bonnie, and many others who were instrumental in editing this work. I haven't worked with any editor aside from my regular one in many, many years, but it was quite refreshing, and your suggestions made the book much better, so thank you.

In "real life," I'm an older woman, so to get into the head of Alex, I needed some help, so I want to acknowledge the people who were the models for the character, Alex. They don't want to be named for the same reasons I'm writing under a pseudonym, but each was so forthcoming and shared their souls with me. To the extent that I got the young millennial mindset right, it was because of their honesty and authenticity. With young people like them doing their work, the kids will be alright.

About the Authors

DR. DAN ENGLE

Dr. Dan Engle is a psychiatrist with a clinical practice that combines aspects of regenerative medicine, psychedelic research, integrative spirituality, and peak performance.

His medical degree is from the University of Texas in San Antonio, his Psychiatry Residency degree is from the University of Colorado in Denver, and his Child and Adolescent Psychiatry Fellowship degree is from Oregon Health and Sciences University.

He is the founder and Medical Director of Kuya, the Institute for Transformational Medicine in Austin, Texas, and Full Spectrum Medicine, a psychedelic integration and educational platform. He is also a consultant to Onnit Labs in Austin and several international healing centers using long-standing indigenous plant medicines for healing and awakening.

www.drdanengle.com
www.fullspectrummedicine.com
www.kuya.life

ALEX YOUNG

Alex Young is the pen name for a well-known bestselling novelist who, due to the still-not-quite-legal nature of MDMA therapy, wishes to remain anonymous.